*For my mother
and in memory of my father*

∾ HEATHER REYES ∾

Heather Reyes is the author of two novels, *Zade* (published by Saqi Books and longlisted for the 2006 Prince Maurice Prize) and *Miranda Road* (2014). She has edited nine anthologies of writing about world cities for Oxygen Books' *city-pick* series. Her short stories and articles have appeared in a wide variety of publications, in the UK and USA, and she is author of four illustrated books for children.

www.heatherreyes.co.uk

∽ FOREWORD ∽

Although this little book about reading was written in the context of serious illness, it is hoped that books rather than illness will be the main focus of the reader's attention.

To avoid cluttering the text with the dates and publication details of the books mentioned, these can be found in the 'Selected Bibliography' at the end of the volume.

Deepest thanks to our wonderful NHS, as well as to my loving, supportive family and friends – above all to Malcolm, without whom ...

Books, like love, can make one little room 'an everywhere'.

I couldn't go out much for a while – apart from trips to the hospital. If the treatment went well, this would just be temporary, but I had some months of near-incarceration to get through.

In the beginning the high doses of chemotherapy affected my eyes so I couldn't see to read properly. All I could do was lie on the bed and listen to chamber music (too delicate for symphonic or jazz or world). Determined to direct my mind away from what was going on in my body, I listened with more attention than I had done for years, discovering small beauties I'd never noticed in familiar Beethoven quartets, detecting extra humour in Satie, noting some spine-tingling key changes in Bartok – and at the same time observing, with a laugh at myself, how the mind could focus on such details, to the point of preciousness, in its desperation to ignore the flesh … of which it's a part.

But it was this experience of increased richness and expansion to be got from 'reduced circumstances' that saved me from – or at least mitigated – a good deal of the anguish attending my suddenly changed situation, and also helped me through the physical difficulties. As soon as the chemo dose was lowered to something nearer what my body could cope with, I got my eyes back and began to read – read as I hadn't had time to for years.

So, in one respect, my 'new situation' presented itself as a luxury, an indulgence, an opportunity. In my puritan-work-ethic family, anyone reading a novel in the morning – reading *anything* apart from the newspaper, briefly, over breakfast – was morally suspect. Even my mother, having discovered – in her eighties – the joy of large print library books, once confessed with guilt-laden voice to sometimes reading a little of her novel *straight after breakfast*. And at first it did feel strange to be able to read whatever I wanted – not for teaching or writing or editing or research – all day long, picking about in world literature, classics, recent publications on all kinds of topics, just as the mood took me. And for the first time I thanked God for Amazon. I've always loved traditional bookshops: I love handling books, I love browsing and the seren-dipitous discoveries that often result. But my browsing days would be on hold for a while. I'd have to rely on reviews, the recommendations of friends, and what was already lurking, unread, on our bookshelves.

My partner, Malcolm, was with me when I was given the totally unexpected diagnosis the afternoon before we were due to go to southern France for a late, much-needed week's holiday by the sea. I lay awake and shook all night, the numbers 4 and 5 doing a Witches' Sabbath of a dance before my eyes: when I'd asked, that afternoon, 'How long have I got?', my consultant had given a Gallic-style shrug and said, with bleak medical honesty, 'Four or five years … ' – though he did add (perhaps noting how the blood had rushed to my face or had drained totally from it) ' … but you're young. It could be longer.' And the nurse added, 'We do have a couple of people still walking about ten or twelve years after diagnosis.' But it was that initial 'Four or five' that stuck. And, dancing alongside those numbers were all the things I wasn't going to see and do after all: unlike my own parents, I wouldn't be in my grandchildren's graduation photos, their wedding photos … wouldn't hold my great-grandchildren. Wouldn't write all the books I'd had plans for. Wouldn't travel with Malcolm to all the places we still hadn't experienced together …

But the night's anguish also produced what was possibly a chemically-driven energy and determination to live as much and as intensely as possible while I could and, despite not a minute's sleep, I was up and ready for our 8 a.m. taxi. And I tried to

tell myself it wouldn't necessarily be the last time I'd
board our beloved Eurostar to Paris.

We'd decided to stop overnight in Paris (a small, basic
hotel right next to the Sorbonne: from our bedroom
window we could see seminars in progress), giving
us a sun-drenched autumn afternoon to walk around
some of our favourite places. We had coffee among
the fallen leaves in the Luxembourg Gardens and
picked up some books to 'get us through to our next
trip', we agreed, with determined optimism.

Our favourite Paris bookshops include the small
'L'Arbre du voyageur' on the rue Mouffetard (rather
cramped, but with high-quality, wonderfully-chosen
stock and classical music played at just the right
volume) and the larger 'La Hune' in Saint Germain.
And it was to 'La Hune' that we went with a certain
sense of much-repeated ritual, of fondling a kind of
intellectual comfort blanket. In the heart of the Latin
Quarter, a few steps from the cafés Flore and Deux
Magots – where Sartre, de Beauvoir *et al* used to go to
write and talk – 'La Hune' (which means 'crow's nest':
I like to think of it as a nautical metaphor for the long
distances that can be 'seen' through books) doesn't
have the supermarket feel that you get in some of the
big chains in Britain and the USA, of books as just
another consumer product – and the stock combines

breadth, depth, all the literature standards as well as attention drawn to new publications.

Unsure whether the small Mediterranean town of Collioure (our destination) would be well-served with bookshops, and knowing our return trip through Paris wouldn't allow time for buying (and we didn't know how long my treatment would keep us from travelling) we indulged ourselves more generously than usual. We could have bought the same things in one of London's French bookshops (or ordered them from French Amazon), but it was just *nicer* to buy them in Paris, even if it did mean weighing our bags down with them for the rest of the holiday. It was worth it. And anyway, we didn't really know which books we wanted until we saw them.

Those plain cream paper covers with nothing but the title, author and, discreetly small, the name of the publisher: there's something so proudly French about them. They don't insult the reader. No attempt to lure with a slick or arty illustration; assuming you will know what you want to buy because you've read the reviews or had the book recommended by a friend, or that you already know the author's work and will pounce on any new publication bearing their name. Or perhaps that in itself is the lure: intellectual flattery. And of course a number of them bear a red paper band announcing a prize recently won by the book or its author. I'm a sucker for those plain cream covers. That day I collected a small pile of them ... then added some cheaper Livre de Poche-style paperbacks with shiny, colourful covers.

Next morning, with our stash of books crammed into our cases, guaranteeing multiple creasings in the week's clothes, we took an early taxi to the Gare de Lyon and had time for breakfast on the station. Great atmosphere. The excitement of long-distance travel and a misty-ish view down the platforms made us think of Monet's painting of the Gare d'Austerlitz. With difficulty I pushed down half a croissant and only managed the coffee in sips. The shock of the diagnosis had killed my all-too-healthy appetite stone dead.

Then the TGV journey down through France. I love trains. My one-time ambition of travelling the entire length of the Trans-Siberian Railway was unlikely to be realised now, but I'd make the most of short-range substitutes ... like the TGV.

Between periods of gazing out of the window and trying to catch the names of stations as we sped through, I read one of the smallest books (right size for lap-bag) bought the previous day – Henri Troyat's *Aliocha*, a brief but moving and heavily autobiographical novel (in fact the nearest thing to an autobiography he ever wrote) about the son of Russian emigrés in Paris.

I knew Henri Troyat (he died in 2007, aged ninety-five) from his biography of Tolstoy. It's very long and I'd never have got through it in French so I am very grateful to Nancy Amphoux who undertook the demanding task of translating it. I'm ashamed to say I haven't read any of his other many biographies of great Russian literary and historical figures and I only knew one of his novels – *La Neige en deuil*, an unforgettable story of a plane crash in the Alps and of the attempt of a tender-hearted but simple-minded character to save the life of an Indian woman. (Subsequent and abiding terror of flying over the Alps: the power of literature … if you let it get to you.) But I'm interested in the lives of emigrés so am pleased my bookshop browsing found me *Aliocha*.

Aliocha's parents and their Russian friends can think only of returning to their old life in Russia. They invest every small twist and turn of post-Revolution political events there with a significance that supports their belief that such a return to the past will be possible. But it's a way of life that means nothing to their children who want to be part of the new culture in which they find themselves, looking to the future rather than being anchored in the past, loving – as Aliocha does – their new language, their new country, and determined to be accepted as part of it.

Although dealing with the specific immigrant situation of Russian exiles in Paris post-1917, Aliocha's experiences are probably shared by many children of modern immigrants and refugees – the older adults anchored in their past and in another place, with a set of customs they are anxious for their children to share ... or which, in some cases, they attempt to impose upon their children who wish to blend in with and take advantage of their adoptive country and culture. The opposite can sometimes be true, of course: some parents wish their children to be part of the adopted culture while the children, feeling beleaguered in a sometimes unsympathetic host nation, try to acquire a strong sense of group identity by vigorously asserting their original culture. (The issue of the Islamic veil, particularly in France, is a case in point.) More often however, adaptation is, for the young, a matter of survival. They need to pull away from their parents, just as the young in general need to assert themselves against the culture and expectations of their parents who grew up in a different world and who often feel threatened by the challenge of their children's different values and propensities. *Aliocha* raises such general issues even while seeming to be about a young Russian boy in Paris – just as any book worth reading speaks to its readers of more than its surface subject and concerns, inviting them to relate it to their life and experiences, provoking comparisons, reflection, awareness.

Aliocha also contains a story of the personal love, and loss, of a close friend. It reminded me of Simone de Beauvoir's loss of her close friend Zaza in *Memoirs of a Dutiful Daughter*, and even more painfully of Bérénice, a much loved and admired friend of mine who'd died suddenly at the age of twenty-two. Even if I only make sixty-six, I will have had her life-span three times over, I told myself. But I wasn't yet ready for the dubious comfort of rationality: it wasn't even forty-eight hours since I'd been given the diagnosis.

I hadn't quite finished *Aliocha* when we had to change trains at Perpignan, taking the little branch line that goes through Collioure – our destination – before it goes on over the nearby border into Spain.

∾ TWO ∾

We fell in love with Collioure at once. It was easy to see why Matisse had loved to paint there. 'The light, and so much else'.[1] Our hotel was virtually on the beach and our balcony overlooked the small, sheltered bay lined with an ancient citadel and church and a pell-mell of white-walled, orange-roofed houses. Too lovely not to be crowded in summer. But it was off-season. The place was still far from empty (quite a lot of early retired from the Home Counties and those, like us, no longer bound to the wheel of school holidays), but there was always plenty of space on the beach and free tables at the outdoor restaurants, where it was still warm enough to eat, even in the late evening.

On leaving our hotel the first morning, we immediately encountered a funeral party – a modest crocodile of people in black, heads bowed, walking slowly in the direction of the ancient church. A scene from a Greek or Italian movie … It wasn't really what I needed. We averted our eyes and walked on to the

---

1   Actually the title of a 1931 painting, by Paul Klee: but it just seemed right here.

centre of town to buy tickets for the little tourist train we'd read about in the guide book, recommended as a way of getting a general overview of the place.

The 'train' started from the town centre and followed a rough road-track up into the hills. It provided an incongruous touch of Disney in the otherwise authentic old port. Swaying and bumping its way ever higher, it gave us precipitous views of valleys cultivated since pre-Roman times – as the crackly, scarcely audible recorded commentary informed us, to the inescapable accompaniment of the American woman behind us, telling her friend, in excruciating detail, about some incident that had occurred at San Francisco airport. (Was it cowardice or the triumph of civilised behaviour that stopped me from turning around and telling her to '*shut the f— up* and let me enjoy the view as I might never see it again'?)

And suddenly I realised I wasn't afraid, even though we were so close to where the ground fell away steeply. It was the kind of trip that would normally have turned me white-knuckled with anxieties. How safe was it? Did the driver really know what he was doing? He was a big man and sweating profusely: was he going to have a heart-attack? Did the brakes operate on the principle of the 'dead man's handle'? And how often were the brakes checked?

How crumbly was the ground near the edge...? A strong survival instinct lay behind such anxiety – the same instinct that had always led me to avoid air and ferry (and even car) travel whenever possible. But all that had evaporated like a mist before the powerful sunshine of a possibly looming eternity. I was left with the most incredible sense of lightness and freedom. Totally unexpected. *The Unbearable Lightness of Being.* (The title of Milan Kundera's novel screeched in my head.) And I was suddenly sure that, if the treatment gave me a long enough remission and good enough health, I might finally have the courage to go to Istanbul ... St Petersburg ... Athens ... San Francisco ... and other places one had to leave *terra firma* in order to visit.

Rather than scaring me, the alarming bump and sway and precipitous descent of the silly train was sheer pleasure. I wanted to laugh all the time. Was I slightly hysterical or light-headed from lack of food and sleep? I'd stared at the dim light from the gap between the curtains all night and listened to the sea. Two consecutive nights awake.

The notion that my condition might somehow be turned into an *opportunity* – rather than remaining only the curse it obviously was – began to flicker, if dimly, in a little corner of my death-panicked brain. Perhaps I was already entering the period of acceptance and adaptation my consultant had hinted at …

On the second morning, ambling around the bay towards the entrance to the great cliffy citadel of the 'Château Royal', we heard music and saw a loose crocodile of brightly-dressed people. Not a funeral, this time, but a wedding party, a small jazz band leading bride, groom and guests in a modest parade around the town, inviting the smiles and good wishes of locals and tourists alike. Again, it was such a Mediterranean scene, it could equally be taking place in some out-of-the-way part of Spain, Italy, Greece … We watched, smiled our happiness for the couple. It was the day I got my appetite back.

That night, I finally slept … only to wake in the early hours sobbing from a nightmare. Another woman was after Malcolm and let it show: I screamed, 'It's only two days since my diagnosis: at least you two could wait till I'm *dead!* It won't be *that* long.' Then I found some kind of notebook in which my beloved had copied out some beautiful quotations, obviously for me, from the books he'd been reading … which reassured me it was a one-sided attraction and that the woman was malicious … until I read the dedication in the front of the notebook: it was to *her*. So, they just couldn't wait for me to die. Such utter, utter desolation. I began to sob … and woke myself up. He took me in his arms until I calmed down. 'Sorry,' I said, 'I had a nightmare.' But I didn't elaborate. A deep fear had conspired with the details of the day to deliver the little horror story: the wedding, reading, him getting changed under a very small towel on the beach and a solitary woman sunbathing nearby just happening to turn her head towards him at the crucial moment …

Even the sleeping brain is an organ for producing narratives.

Over breakfast we talked a bit about this and how it's no different, really, from what the very much awake brains of writers do: their own experiences and knowledge and observations are fragments of coloured plastic in the end of a kaleidoscope which they twist to make a pattern, turning a fraction this way and that till they come up with a satisfying design. They pass the tube carefully on to us so we can put our eye to the viewing hole: hopefully the pattern will not have slipped as we take it and that what we see is the pattern prepared for us – more or less. One of the interesting aspects of reading writers' biographies is recognising how elements from their life have entered their work, and reflect on the ways in which they have patterned them into a narrative that is useful to the reader, something of general relevance made from the specifics of their lives. We come up with some examples as we finish our coffee: George Eliot's relationship with her brother played out as Maggie and Tom Tulliver in *The Mill on the Floss*; the 'pointless' death (from typhoid) of Virginia Woolf's beloved brother Toby turned into a lament for all the young men lost in the First World War in *Jacob's Room*. But we didn't get any further than these: the sun was shining, the Mediterranean glittering; I'd slept; I'd eaten; the nightmare was beginning to fade ... though I dreaded going to sleep the next night in case my frightened brain came up with more nasty little stories.

But it didn't.

For the whole week the weather remained balmy, the October sea still swimmable (though not for me). We took breakfast outside each morning and ate lunch and dinner at outdoor restaurants with good-humoured waiters – lots of anchovies and sardines ... and I made the most of the red wine: I'd soon have to stay off it for a while.

A few steps behind our hotel was the paradoxically ancient building of the Musée d'Art Moderne, showing a collection of Matisse drawings. Exquisite! I'd always loved his work but had only learnt to appreciate it more thoroughly after reading Hilary

Spurling's prize-winning biography and visiting the Royal Academy's exhibition, curated by Spurling herself, focusing on his inspiration from textiles. It had been a revelation, relating the riotous colour of the paintings to Matisse's origins in a textile town and his own collection of materials and costumes – though I remain just as fond of the pared-down simplicity and subtlety of the drawings. The pleasure of a haiku rather than a novel.

Behind the Musée is a sense-delighting walk through sloping olive groves, up to a restored wind-mill that could have come straight out of *Don Quixote* (we were, after all, just a stone's throw from the Spanish border).

Once you've read *Don Quixote*, a windmill is no longer just a windmill; it reverberates with one of the most memorably comic (and oddly heartbreaking) scenes in the whole of literature – the well-meaning but mad old knight, Don Quixote de la Mancha, mistaking some windmills for a breed of up-to-no-good giants striding over the landscape and, charging them, lance in hand, to rid the world of evil, but getting caught up in the turning sails and being whisked up into the air.

You could, I suppose, conclude that such associations are intrusive, or get in the way of the simple immediacy of an experience. Personally, I think they

enhance it. Why not enjoy the 'value added' quality
of an experience that gathers around itself references
from literature and art? – references that help one see
more fully and so with more pleasure. I remember
an increased delight in the pink-and-white variety
of hawthorn blossom after reading Proust's description of it as crushed strawberries in cream cheese.
(That's exactly it!) The human brain is hard-wired to
'make connections': it's how we survive and operate
in the world, so we're programmed to take pleasure
in comparisons, metaphors, links of any kind.

But it's true that books *can* get in the way of life.
It's Don Quixote's obsession with the stories he's
read that shapes the way he sees the world and his
expectations of it – just as Flaubert's Emma Bovary
is destroyed by trying to make her life match the
glamour and excitement she's encountered in novels;
and just as Catherine Morland, in Jane Austen's
Northanger Abbey, is made to look foolish when her
reading of Gothic novels leads to a grave misinter-
pretation of people and situations.

The problem for poor old Don Quixote is that the
books he's read have nothing to do with the reali-
ties of the world of his time – they're old-fashioned,
chivalric romances. They're simply not useful narratives for 'thinking the world' as it actually is. *Don
Quixote* (along with *Madame Bovary* and *Northanger*

Abby) underlines the powerful effects of reading – 'we are what we read' – and suggests the need for discrimination in the books we expose ourselves to. Reading nothing but James Bond novels or endlessly re-reading Harry Potter to the exclusion of all else will reduce our minds to those single visions and sets of experiences and vocabularies. It matters *what* we read, not just *that* we read. As Beattie says (quoting her lover and mentor), in Arnold Wesker's play *Roots*, 'There's nothing wrong with comics only there's something wrong with comics all the time. There's nothing wrong with football, only there's something wrong with *only* football.'

And the same goes for more 'serious' books. Damage done to the world by people who read only one book, whether it's the Bible, the Koran, the Talmud, or the Communist Manifesto, may be greater than by those who read nothing at all but listen carefully to the spoken words of many different others. We need to encourage 'people of books' rather than 'people of The Book'. This is not to denigrate the wisdom and interest to be found in the great books of religion, but it is more helpful, I think, to build the book of ourselves, to construct our world view, with the help of as many varied voices as possible. We need to read the Bible *and* the Koran *and* the Talmud … and lots and lots of other books, too.

In front of me on my desk, as I am writing this, is

a card from my daughter – a drawing of some very small people among shelves and shelves and shelves of books: the caption is 'LAWS OF NATURE #13: There's no such thing as too many books.' (Another 'LAW OF NATURE' might be 'The number of books you have will always exceed the space on your bookshelves' – though we haven't yet taken to piling them on the sides of the stairs as suggested in *Living with Books*, a gift from my son: there's a 'health and safety' issue there – one's neck is more precious than books).

Yes, everyone should have lots and lots of books! Just as World Music has hugely enriched the soundscape of contemporary music of all kinds, so we can all build richer selves by opening our minds to as many 'differences' as possible. We should try to make great cosmopolitan cities of ourselves, not poky-if-comfortable little towns in the middle of nowhere.

We always take an over-optimistic number of books on holiday. They're unpacked, lined up on whatever convenient surface the hotel room affords, marking our temporary territory … then neglected while we read new books bought locally. This time we hadn't packed too many, knowing we intended to pick some up in Paris.

On the second night we unpacked our 'La Hune' purchases (a bit like Christmas: we'd forgotten half of what we'd bought) and turned the spacious but rather soulless hotel room into more than a place for drying off beach-wear.

I flicked through each one, trying to decide what to read next, now I'd finished *Aliocha*, weighing up what would suit my mood and our location.

Daniel Pennac's *Chagrin d'école*? Maybe. I'd read and enjoyed his *Comme un roman*, the back cover of which, instead of a promotional blurb, gives a list of the inalienable rights of the reader – giving a taste of his general 'take' on things: these rights include the right not to read, the right to skip, to not finish a book, to read anything, to mistake a book for real life, to read anywhere ... Pennac is one of those writers who can handle 'the serious' with a gracious lightness of touch that is utterly charming. Though I was looking forward to *Chagrin d'école* enormously, I didn't specially want to enter the fraught world of education while on holiday.

What about Muriel Barbery's *L'Élégance du hérisson*? It had been a serendipitous choice. And it also had one of the red bands drawing attention to its having won the 'Prix des Libraires'. There was the sound of the title, too – the repeated 'e acute' sound of '*élégance*' combined with the two soft sounds of 'ce' and 'ss' and the liquid 'rr' ... was that it? And the title was, of course, intriguing: 'The Elegance of the

Hedgehog'. (Not quite so mellifluous in English!) But it was longish: three hundred and fifty-six pages. Of French? For a beach read? I don't think so.

Maybe J. M. G. Le Clézio's *Raga: approche du continent invisible* would be more suitable. It promised to be a fascinating portrait of Oceania – a Pacific 'continent' of islands. I'd discovered Le Clézio years ago when the English translation of *Terra Amata* was being virtually given away in one of the bargain bins my youthful poverty encouraged me to haunt. The 'Prologue' to *Terra Amata*, addressed to the reader, is about the act of reading. Some years later, when I read Italo Calvino's *If on a Winter's Night a Traveller*, I felt the opening was somehow familiar. But it was a while before I identified the source of the echo. Both are amusing passages about the choosing and reading of books, the tone somehow similar though written more than a decade apart (*Terra Amata* in 1967, *If on a Winter's Night a Traveller* in 1979) and in different languages. Books sometimes make strange friendships between themselves.

Most readers would find something of themselves in those extracts from Le Clézio and Calvino; they're worth searching out if you want something to make you smile with recognition. One of the sections from the Calvino passage I especially recall is his description of going into a bookshop and being frowned at by all the books you haven't read. He tells the reader not any account to be awed by them, because there are acres and acres of books you needn't read for various reasons. But when safely beyond these ramparts, you're attacked by 'the infantry of the Books That If You Had More Than One Life You Would Certainly Also Read But Unfortunately Your Days Are Numbered'. When I'd first read it, in my thirties, the last phrase had no particular significance for me. Now, of course, it jumps out and hits me in the face with more force than Calvino probably intended (or maybe he did: I don't know). And this reminds me that it's good to read favourite books at different times of life: they speak to us in different ways according to 'where we are' in life, and what we have experienced. Yes, it's good to re-read ... if you have time.

Back to that little stash of plain-covered books I was arranging on a shelf in the hotel room ... Nobel prize-winner Claude Simon's *La Chevelure de Bérénice* is a mere twenty-four expensive pages, but I grab anything by Simon. The extra enticement is the title. (Titles: just one of the reasons for choosing books.) Bérénice – the lost friend I mentioned earlier: the first truly intelligent, educated and beautiful person I'd known, idol of my childhood and youth. But I don't want her name continually before my eyes at the moment.

Another short book we'd picked up in Paris was *Gare du Nord* by Abdelkader Djemaï. It follows, the blurb says, the difficulties and pleasures of three immigrants, now retired, living in Paris. I hadn't read his previous books and I can't remember why this one caught my attention, but the previous autumn, as part of a research project, we'd been in Paris for the annual *Lire en fête* book festival that takes place throughout France, and had gone to one or two events featuring writers who had written of their experiences as immigrants. I'd made a resolution then to try to read more of these important voices. And this was one of them. But probably not a good beach read. Too urban.

Although I love Boris Vian, I'd bought *Contes de fées à l'usage des moyennes personnes* more to complete my collection of his work than for immediate reading and didn't feel in the mood for his verbal and narrative playfulness at that moment. Vian was originally part of the Sartre-de Beauvoir set, only much nicer than most of them, and certainly a lot funnier – though he wasn't amused when Sartre effectively broke up his marriage by having an affair with his wife. Vian was one of those multi-talented, prolific people racing against what he knew was likely to be an early death. He'd lived with a heart problem since childhood and died of a heart attack at thirty-seven after watching a film preview of his novel *J'ai irai cracher sur vos tombes* ('I'll spit on your graves') of which he disapproved.

Vian's novels are utterly unique (the later ones very different from *J'irai cracher*) – funny, weird, charming. He was also a trumpeter and an important figure in the post-war jazz scene, not only for his prolific jazz journalism but for actively promoting American jazz musicians in Paris. But best of all are his songs: he wrote hundreds. Wonderful songs with such a range of subjects and emotions that there are always new joys and jokes to discover, from the poignancy and anger of *À tous les enfants* to the savage satire of *Les joyeux buchers* and the atmospheric charm and humour of *Rue Watt*, describing a walk and conversation in this down-at-heel road with his friend, the writer Raymond Queneau. Unfortunately, because of Vian's use of word-play and French colloquial idioms, the songs don't translate well into English – and the referential contexts tend to be specifically French, too. (Access to Vian is just one of the reasons I am perennially grateful to that slightly odd French teacher of mine who drilled us so thoroughly in vocab and grammar.) Happily, Vian's novels *have* been translated.

Most of Raymond Queneau has been translated, too. He's another extraordinarily original, funny and totally charming writer, probably best known for

Zazie dans le métro. (Louis Malle's wonderful film of it is a good place to start, though the book's even better.) Once met on the page, Zazie and her unforgettable Uncle Gabriel – not to mention the parrot – will stay with you for ever. As with Vian, I'd bought his *Contes et propos* to fill a hole in my library: 'something for later'.

Erik Orsenna might be a pleasant and not too demanding read. I'd discovered him through a glowing review of one of his children's books, *Le Grammaire est une chanson douce*. (He's since followed this with further original and charming little books on other aspects of language – such as the use of the subjunctive, and another on accented letters – though they're unlikely to be translated as they refer specifically to French usage.) I haven't yet tried his novels, but enjoyed his small book on the famous seventeenth-century garden designer André Le Nôtre, *Portrait d'un homme heureux*, and was looking forward to this latest purchase, *Portrait du Gulf Stream*. It's a toss-up between this and Le Clézio's book on Oceania … which is what I go for in the end. It should be good for reading on the beach at Collioure, with the foothills of the Pyrenees rising in the background …

I didn't in the end do much reading during that

week in Collioure, except at night, back at the hotel, if there wasn't anything good on French TV. Even on the beach, my reading was spasmodic, desultory. I found I just wanted to live in the moment, to 'be', to enjoy the physical immediacy of the sun, the sea, the beauty, the food. Storing it up for later. And needing time to think, to come to terms with the fact that, even if the treatment were successful for a while, I wasn't, after all, likely to live to the ripe old age enjoyed by most of the women in my family. (Perhaps I had too many genes from my dear paternal grandfather who'd died of cancer at sixty-seven.) The word 'longevity' had always sounded a bit clumsy and irritating to me: now it was a coveted jewel of the greatest price. (Words, as well as books, can change their meanings for us according to 'where we are' in life.)

Panic and sadness.

Then more helpful thoughts broke through. What was the point of nearly half a century's reading and thinking if, when it came to the basic crunch situation of one's mortality, it provided no help?

Wasn't being a reader one of the ways to achieve a continual awareness of other people's lives, of what was happening elsewhere than in one's own little world? In lives that are fairly restricted – like the lives of most of us – reading has to replace the breadth of actually lived experience that can develop this wider awareness. In E. M. Forster's *Howards End*, Helen Schlegel says to her sister, Margaret, 'You meant to keep proportion, and that's heroic ...' Keep proportion. Keep yourself and your own life in perspective, I tell myself. Be heroic. That's what people are expecting ... Not that anyone apart from myself, Malcolm and the consultant yet know that I have cancer. We'll tell family and friends gradually, once we get back to England and have had time to come to terms with it ourselves. Hardest will be telling the children ...

'Keep proportion.' Perspective. Yes, I was indeed fortunate if my destiny was to die of a disease at twice the life-expectancy age of some African countries; to die, probably in bed, with the help of pain relief, rather than be hacked to death in some unimaginably horrific genocide; fortunate not to be dying young, of AIDS, in some comfortless shack in South Africa, without ameliorating drugs. And, really, I'd already lived a long time compared with Mozart (who died at thirty-five), Mendelssohn and Mayakovsky (thirty-six), Pushkin and Boris Vian (thirty-seven). I had two marvellous children and three amazing grandchildren. I'd had a career, a lot of happiness, a lot of love. Time passes. We all have to die ...

But it's hard. I'm happy. I enjoy life. I'd prefer it to

end later rather than sooner.

Maybe it will.

Meantime, live. And, as Flaubert wrote to Mademoiselle de Chantepie in June 1857, 'Read in order to live'. To live more richly. If you can't go out into the world, bring the world to you.

The destination of the Collioure 'fun train' we'd taken on the first morning, before descending and returning via the next small town along the coast, had been an old hill-top fort, visible from almost everywhere in Collioure and more-or-less directly behind our hotel, reachable via a continuation of the same path that took one to the 'Don Quixote windmill'. Should we try it?

It was near the end of our week and I was feeling stronger, more relaxed, and had finally got some (nightmareless) sleep. It'd be a steep climb, quite rocky and uneven. I wasn't sure I could make it. I said I'd go a little way, then sit and wait while Malcolm went to the top. Stopping for a bit to catch my breath, I decided I could go a bit further ... then a bit further ... And, suddenly deciding not to be beaten, breathing hard and legs wobbly, made it to the top.

Worth every step! Not just for the sense of achievement, of still being healthy enough to do it, and not just for the magnificent views, but for the *smells*. The delicate odour of wild herbs; the heavier, sweet scent of bushes we couldn't identify; and the resiny pines. Everywhere the life of the senses enhanced. No wonder Matisse had loved it so much.

I've met people who assume the life of the mind is somehow in opposition to the life of the senses. Put at its crudest, that those who read a lot probably don't enjoy sex. The evidence (both historical and personal) is to the contrary. Examples spring immediately to mind of some famous female intellectuals: Heloïse (twelfth century), Mme du Châtelet (eighteenth century), Georges Sand (nineteenth century), Simone de Beauvoir (twentieth century). Their male counterparts have a more obvious reputation for enjoying bodily pleasures: no need to spend space on them here.

Impossible to know how others experience smell, taste, touch, colour, but the life of the senses can be enhanced by reading. Or should be if it's properly undertaken and involves the right *kind* of reading. The wrong kind blunts the senses by immersing the reader in clichés and banalities.

And this is where I find poetry important. The attention to freshness and accuracy, the illuminating links set up by insightful and surprising metaphors that are the hallmarks of most worthwhile poetry are a largely neglected resource (if the sales and promotion of poetry are anything to go by). And, as I said earlier, metaphor is known to be a most valuable process in the development of thinking and awareness: the ability to 'make connections'. (E. M. Forster again – that epigraph to *Howards End*: 'Only connect'.)

I always mean to read more poetry. But it requires the kind of slow, concentrated attention that I couldn't muster just then. I needed to rush and wallow and immerse myself quickly in all manner of other worlds. Poetry would be for later, when I was feeling better ... apart from the wonderful poems sent (at my request) by two friends, Jeremy Over and Marita Over, whose work is full of delicacy, shadows, intelligence and delight.

We took only one trip outside Collioure during our week there – a train across the Spanish border to Port Bou, a pilgrimage to the grave of Walter Benjamin, the Jewish philosopher, philologist, literary critic and political commentator. A champion of Bertolt Brecht's work, Benjamin left Germany for Paris with the rise of Nazism, where he began a vast study of the city as it was in the nineteenth-century. On the German invasion of France, he tried to flee to Spain but, denied official entry and convinced he was about to be arrested by the Gestapo, he committed suicide at Port Bou, so close to freedom.

We found Port Bou rather ugly, run-down, and unpleasant. Terrible things had gone on in the area at the end of the Spanish Civil War: one could imagine it. The one positive moment was an encounter with a very nice lady dusting shelves and ornaments in the cramped but cosy cemetery, for all the world as if it were her sitting-room. ('Death where is thy sting? Grave where is thy mystery? ... ') She directed us to Benjamin's humble resting place. Despite her lack of English and our lack of Spanish, we got along famously.

When Hannah Arendt – also a Jewish political philosopher and a great admirer of Benjamin – visited that little cemetery, high on its hill overlooking the sea, she considered it the most beautiful place in the world. To us it seemed impossibly bleak and depressing. The Walter Benjamin monument (not far from the cemetery) is a terrifying oblong tunnel of rusty metal heading steeply down the hillside with a far-end view straight into a seethe of sea. In the circumstances of Benjamin's death, perhaps bleakness and terror were more appropriate than beauty.

I couldn't wait to get away from the sadness and death and run-downness of Port Bou (it had been a thriving customs post before the European borders came down) and back to the beauty of Collioure

– though the renewed contact with Benjamin made me feel a little guilty that, despite admiring him and liking other things I'd read by him, I hadn't got very far when I'd tried to tackle his great (though unfinished) and fascinating doorstep of a book, a study of nineteenth-century Paris known as *The Arcades Project*. I couldn't remember why I'd abandoned it after a couple of dozen pages, even though it was the English translation we had (and what a task that must have been to translate it!). Had it just been too heavy to hold? … or was the print too small or badly spaced? … Maybe the physical qualities of a book are not always taken sufficiently into account. Maybe it just wasn't the right time. Or did the investment of time required seem out of proportion to what I, personally, was likely to get out of it? I was even less likely to persist with it now.

(Apologies, Benjamin.)

Gratitude for the early morning and greyness and the beginnings of rain as we dragged our cases to the station. I'd rarely been so regretful at leaving a place: a sunny morning would have made the going worse.

But in Paris the late afternoon *was* sunny. From the Gare de Lyon we walked through the Jardin des Plantes. We'd been going to Paris for years before visiting the Jardin for the first time … finally led there by a book: Claude Simon's *Le Jardin des Plantes*. It became one of our favourite places. And it was particularly beautiful that October day, the warmer than usual autumn allowing flowers to go on blooming everywhere, the paths walked by the usual mixture of elegant older Parisians, mothers with ebullient children, tourists, students. And I cried – for the first time since the diagnosis (not counting the nightmare). Cried with the beauty of the place and the anguish of suddenly wondering if this would be my last visit, felt sorry for myself and all my plans that might never be completed and for all the associations of previous visits. Cried for all the beauty in the world and for the loveliness of a paragraph in that book by Simon, taken from the name of the place, describing the colours of the saris worn by a class of girls sitting in a circle at an Indian school of music and dance – saris the colours of flowers and fruits: '*géranium, indigo, carmine, pervenche, cerise, pourpre, safran, grenat, vieux rose, citron, réséda ...*' (Those colours! I wanted to see them for ever ...) Cried, and had to be cuddled ...

... though only for about half a minute. I pulled myself together, found my sun-glasses to cover my eyes, and we went off to find a Chinese restaurant, where we had a splendid meal before catching our Eurostar back to London.

∾ THREE ∾

First week of chemotherapy. *Ghastly*. A massive cocktail of tablets.

I live with a sense of hideous immediacy every hour of each day, not knowing what my body's going to do next. When I'd asked my consultant how the chemotherapy was likely to affect me, he'd said, 'It depends. Some people can just carry on as normal … going to work or whatever. For some people it's not quite so easy.' Trust me to be right bang up against the furthest extreme of the spectrum: 'Not quite so easy' was nothing if not an understatement.

By the end of the week I'm in hospital, unable even to stand. And I can't see properly: not enough to read. The dose is too strong for a neurotic body like mine. They reduce it. My eyes improve. I can read again – just as well as I can't do much else. I feel too awful to leave the house and, with my legs affected badly on some days, I can't easily get up the stairs to my study. Not that I feel like working … The furthest I go is from my bedroom (it's downstairs) to the sitting-room, with occasional forays to the kitchen.

A kind of imprisonment – incarceration in the very small world of our rather small house … which is, thankfully, very full of books.

And then it dawns on me: my situation is a kind of metaphor for the condition in which we all live all the time – confined to the small room of our own heads and the limited horizons of a single personality and living one, all-too-short life. So I'm not really in a different situation from anyone else: just a bit more so.

Reading as escape from those limiting conditions. But not as escape *from* life: as escape *into* life – a wider, richer, more complex and rewarding life. Drawing life into one little room, into one little head. As much life as possible. Making one little room 'an everywhere'.

Reading as an attempt to cheat Time. By giving ourselves the richness and complexity and differences of reading, whatever time any of us have left to us can be transformed to seem greater – just as the days of our holidays seem an expansion when we're away from our habitual dailinesses and are given (or search out) what is new and different and enriching.

'Bibliotherapy' is nothing new. D. H. Lawrence said, 'One sheds one sicknesses in books', and the critic, Harold Bloom, in *How to Read and Why*, called reading 'the most healing of pleasures'. Wikipedia tells us that, in the USA, it's at least a century old and was particularly well used with soldiers recovering after the Second World War. The books 'kept the patients busy' and were good for their 'general sense of well-being for a variety of reasons' (not given).

But in essence it goes much further back. Even Plato recognised that the arts were an aid to bringing an out-of-tune soul-circuit back into harmony with itself, while it was a common Renaissance idea that poetry and song could rid one of vexations of both the body and the soul. George Eliot alleviated her great grief at the death of her partner by reading Dante, and John Stuart Mill experienced a comparable 'healing' through reading the right book at a difficult time. Though it can just be immersing oneself in literature generally. I have a little anthology called *Thoughts for Book-Lovers* (a third edition, 1904) given to me by a student as a thank you for my 'healthy prescription of enthusiasm for literature', as her carefully-written dedication puts it – though I'm sure I never mentioned the idea of 'bibliotherapy' or 'the reading cure' to my students and sometimes wonder whether the reading I'd tried to encourage had helped her through some particular difficulty ... or whether she simply meant it had enhanced her life in general.

Bibliotherapy has become something of a buzz word recently in certain medical circles, but the actual practice of it is varied. At the most basic level there's the doctor's recommendation that a depressed patient go to the library and read up on their own condition. (I've heard that some doctors have been provided with appropriate reading lists to give patients). The hope is that they will read information and self-help books in order to understand and take control of their condition, with less recourse to medication (I assume this would be mostly for cases of depression or minor ailments resulting from stress). Then there are cancer patients encouraged to join a 'non-cancer group' to discuss 'great books'. And in the most difficult cases, patients with severe, long-term mental illness are being painstakingly coaxed by expert practitioners into language worlds that lay beyond their own closed-in and limiting universe.

In a 2008 *Guardian* article, 'The Reading Cure', Blake Morrison quotes a woman who had suffered from rheumatoid arthritis for thirty years. She found that reading helped to banish the pain to a realm where it no longer seemed important and that entering the world of a book helped her focus on things other than her own problems. In the reading group she joined, members were able, in discussing the books, to deal with subjects usually avoided, such as ageing and death – which was very helpful.

Another woman found that talking about books was more helpful than talking about breast cancer with other women in the same boat. And while it may be of some comfort to read of sufferings that relate to our own experiences, a more profound help can come from entering other worlds that help us place our own in relation to them. Not books that echo or repeat our lives, but those that take us somewhere else.

In *The City of Words*, Alberto Manguel tells the moving story of how a friend of Kafka's beloved Milena,[1] who was with her in the 'mad and meaningless state of brutal suffering' of the concentration camp, attempted to survive the nightmare by resorting to the memory of books read long before, particularly a short story by Gorky, 'A Man is Born', that she had memorised – a story of kindness and simple human goodness. The story offered a place to which she could retreat from the horrors around her. Although it couldn't give meaning to her situation or even offer hope, it provided a balance, a reminder of light in that catastrophic darkness. And it helped her to survive. Such, believes Manguel, is the power of stories.

And, of course, bibliotherapy can simply be sitting on your sofa at home, on your own, reading …

1   Milena Jesenska (1896–1944) first met Kafka in 1919. Eventually they became lovers. A writer, journalist and early feminist, she was his first non-Jewish girlfriend and later his Czech translator, and judging by his letters to her, she was probably the only woman he was ever truly in love with. She died, twenty years after Kafka, in a concentration camp.

So, I sit on the sofa and read books and, because I don't know anyone else who is currently reading the same books as I am, I resort to a conversation about them on paper. I write about them as I go.

It's a long time since I've had the leisure to do this – the leisure to really 'think' at all. And one of the things I begin thinking about is how books came to mean so much to me in the first place, how I 'got into' them … and how it compares with the route of my reading friends. I decide this will be a good topic of conversation when they visit: otherwise we might get stuck with symptoms, treatment etc. *ad nauseam* (and I already have enough 'nausea' in my life, just at the moment: the pills for it are only partially successful).

Each book person has their own distinctive – even idiosyncratic – history, though many share certain general experiences: being read to as a child; particular books received as gifts (at the right time); the example of certain individuals; the contagious enthusiasm of people admired – friends, relatives, teachers … A number of those I ask mention the same books or authors, while others have completely different stories. Age plays a part. One of my former students recalls the impact of Roald Dahl's books on her childhood – their humour and unforgettable villains – and knows she was encouraged to read by receiving books as birthday and Christmas gifts, her love of books leading her to a job in the London Library. A writer friend of my own generation puts her book-love down to being an only child, living in a house with lots of books, and escaping from her friendless condition at boarding school. The lonely mind seeking companionship in books comes up a number of times.

And then there were practical reasons for getting into books – like the friend whose childhood home was right opposite the local library, or those whose parents were teachers and for whom books were as basic to life as bread. The over-fifties often came to Shakespeare, as children, through Charles Lamb's *Tales from Shakespeare* (as I had), while for the under forties it was the Bernard Miles versions. For quite a few, Russian literature had become important to them in their late teens, though none could compete with my Chilean friend who'd read Dostoyevsky's *Crime and Punishment* when she was ten and a half, while confined to bed for several months.

During my survey, some friends asked me about my own reading story, but I was more interested in theirs. (Listening to them also saved me the exhaustion of talking, so I could look forward to visits rather than dreading the fatigue that followed if I had to say too much.)

But here, now, partly for those friends who were kind enough to ask and received no proper reply, are the various ways in which I caught bibliophilia.

> *You spotted snakes with double tongue,*
> *Thorny hedgehogs be not seen ...*

My mother in the old blue armchair by the fire, me sitting on the little leather 'pouffe' by her legs. She doesn't need a 'government initiative' or 'national strategy' to know it's good to read to your children. And, anyway, she loves it. I'm five years old. She's reading from a big red book. A lot of the words I don't understand, but I like the sounds and the rhythms.

> *Quinquireme of Nineveh from distant Ophir*
> *Rowing home to haven in sunny Palestine ...*

For a short time in the 1950s, my godfather and uncle – a gentle, civilised man who introduced me to ballet, Beethoven, and the idea that one could learn a language other than one's own – was an encyclopædia salesman. It didn't last long, perhaps because he was more enthusiastic about the encyclopædias than about selling them. But he did manage to persuade my then quite hard-up parents that what their four-year-old daughter needed most was a set of encyclopædias – Newnes' Pictorial

Knowledge: ten splendid, red-leather-look volumes covering everything from evolution to the history of the police, from Greek mythology to World War II, from the invention of the wheel to the atom bomb. Illustrated mainly with the grainy grey photos of the time, there were a few pages of coloured illustrations in each volume. But they looked peculiar – perhaps the result of some cheap tinting process – and not at all natural. I preferred the black-and-whites. In Volume Nine was a collection of well-known English poems with little black-and-white drawings to illustrate them. Sitting by the fire, hearing the familiar words and rhythms in my mother's gentle voice ...

Then there was *Little Women*, with the still rough, cheap paper of those post-war editions. Jo March, the tom-boy would-be writer who was always reading (modelled on the author, Louisa May Alcott), is everyone's favourite of the four March sisters. I was forever trying to turn the book into a play, typing out the parts endlessly on the little grey 'Lilliput' typewriter I'd been given the Christmas before I was nine. I had visions of acting it with girls from my class, with me playing Jo, of course, my role-model ... and one only superseded, for a time, by Anna Pavlova.

My godfather had taken me to see *The Nutcracker* at the Festival Hall. Hearing how much I'd loved it, my godmother (from the other side of the family) gave me a book called *Dancing Star*, by Gladys Malvern – the story of Anna Pavlova. Whatever its shortcomings as a depiction of the great ballerina's actual life, it was an inspirational story about the dedication and perseverance needed for the creation of great art and was my introduction to Russia and Modernism (one met Diaghilev, the Ballets Russes, Stravinsky …), both important to me later.

They're heroes, people like Gladys Malvern – those who make the wider world available to *children*. Another kind of translation. Like those who make simple arrangements of classical music, enabling children to become familiar with their melodies and rhythms (as I did, and as my very musical little grandson is now doing), giving them a 'way in' to the fuller beauties later on. They have much in common with translators and deserve to be celebrated.

One thing leads to another …

A wet day during a family holiday somewhere on the south coast. A second-hand bookshop: the first time I've been in one. A small section on dance. An old, yellowish-covered book called (in red) *Soviet Ballet* (published, surprisingly, in 1945: I would have thought there were other priorities then!). Along with black and white photos of some predictable Swan Lakes, Sleeping Beauties, Nutcrackers and

Giselles were those of strange, unfamiliar ballets: 'Red Poppy'; 'Baby Stork'; 'Taras Bulba'; 'Prisoner of the Caucasus' … And the long, tongue-twisting Russian names of the dancers: Plesetskaya, Preobrazhensky, Lepeschinskaya, Semyonova, the lines made by their supple bodies so much more beautiful than the stiff and doll-like style of Margot Fonteyn. The lure of the different, the exotic, sewn on to the already known. Russian ballet leading me to Russian music leading me eventually – a hop forward in time – to Russian literature.

A rainy November afternoon. 3.30. The end of an A-level English class in a tiny room at the top of some wooden stairs. A bare bulb above an old table, the room lined with dark-wood shelves on which are arranged all the personal books of the young nun (fresh out of Oxford) who teaches us. She doesn't like teaching us in a classroom: this is 'her' room – a no-longer-used space in the oldest part of the school, a kind of large store-cupboard with a window, known as 'the Print Room' and housing the remains of a primitive hand-press. And we are allowed to borrow any of her books.

There's a Russian section: I can see from the names. Some are very long novels. I'm rather a slow reader. One of the smaller ones is called *Childhood, Boyhood, Youth*: it's by Leo Tolstoy. I borrow it. And

I'm hooked ... Catapulted into a different world, feeling it, living in it.

Pure contingency? Happenstance falling on fertile ground?

From there to *Resurrection*, to *Anna Karenina*, to *War and Peace* and on to Dostoyevsky (though I only get as far as *Crime and Punishment* before the pressures of A-level exams kick in). A girl in my class is reading the poems of Mayakovsky and Yevtushenko. I borrow them after her. I read 'Babi Yar' and begin to discover some of the truths of recent Russian history: it isn't all Tolstoy and ballet.

A point of entry into another world. Drawing other worlds into the self and making it different. Reading.

But by this time I've also made another, quite different reading discovery. Rewind a couple of years: I'm fifteen or sixteen. A book of classroom comprehension passages includes an excerpt from an essay by Montaigne. I can't remember which essay, but there was something in the thoughts that made a big impression on me. Passing a local bookshop soon after, I see the Penguin Classics edition displayed in the window and go in and buy it. If I could only take one book with me to the after-life, this might be it. The first paperback I'd bought for myself: the beginning of my library.

Each time we go to Paris I have to visit the statue of Montaigne in the rue des Écoles and touch his foot. I think many others must do the same: the bronze of his shoe has a well-shined, much-rubbed look. Some may do it for luck, others, like me, out of affection. And he seems amused, sitting there, leaning forward with a smile, as if engaged in a most civilised conversation with you.

But I mustn't forget our primary school library – a small bookcase of mainly fusty old books, among them Charles Lamb's *Tales from Shakespeare*. From this I find out all about that fairy queen near whom those spotted snakes and thorny hedgehogs I'd known since the age of five were not allowed to come. Filling in the picture.

When she hears I've been reading the stories of Shakespeare's plays, the Anna Pavlova aunt gives me, for the Christmas before I turn eleven, *The Complete Works of Shakespeare* – a mass-produced edition on rough paper, the print rather small and smudgily over-black. But it doesn't matter: they're all there – every word of every play. I make my parents read parts with me. We don't always understand what we read, but I like the *idea* of it … and the rhythms and the sounds of the words, their strangeness. And it is a comforting link to those original hours by the fire, at my mother's knee, which I'm now too old for …

Newts and blind worms do no wrong –
Come not near our fairy queen…

For some people, of course, there may be no 'story' of how they came to reading: they're simply from a family where to be a reader is taken for granted. They grow up surrounded by books, by adults who continually read and discuss books, ideas, writers. They may have free access to parental libraries. Reading is just 'what you do'. They are very lucky.

At the other extreme is the African child scratching out letters in the dust, desperate to learn reading, knowing it to be a possible route to survival.

In the 60s, some of the nuns from the school where I was educated and later taught went off to a remote part of northern Kenya and founded a school there. Our English department once sent out some superannuated copies of *Romeo and Juliet* (little square books with shabby blue covers and disintegrating spines), and I remember hearing how the Kenyan teacher broke down in tears when she opened the box and found them. There were enough for each child in the School Certificate class to have a copy. Until then, the teacher had been the only one to possess one ancient, precious copy from which she tried to teach her eager class to the examination standard. (And to think we'd almost binned those books, wondering if it was insulting to send such shabby things.)

It's not only in developing countries that reading and a decent life may go hand in hand. Among those confined in British prisons, at least two-thirds have severe literacy problems. I've known a couple of writers who've worked in prisons, often with those who only acquired the ability to read and write after their incarceration, thanks to the (much under-funded) education programmes for prisoners. And I have heard from those writers how people's lives have been transformed when, through reading, they not only have access to kinds of employment previously beyond their reach, but also learn to enter the experiences of others and, through writing, become able to express their own thoughts and experiences. One of the most moving literary events I've ever attended was the launch of an anthology of poems by young women prisoners. They were allowed to be present (with guards: a couple had done terrible things), reading their own poems to a large and appreciative audience that included the gold-chained local mayor in the front row. As a result of working with the writer, one young woman had been inspired to tackle an 'A' level English course. You can imagine the pride and sense of self-worth it gave those women when it was announced that their anthology had won the Raymond Williams Community Publishing Prize, given annually in memory of the cultural analyst and novelist Raymond Williams (1921-1988), for 'works of outstanding creative and imaginative quality which reflect the voices and experiences of people from different communities across the country'. The writer – poet Cherry Smyth – who had worked with those young women to produce the anthology and to inspire them to read should have her name up in lights.

(I often wonder if the young woman taking her 'A' level English managed to pass.)

∾ FOUR ∾

What have I been reading?

Mainly the books we bought in France. The concentration needed for reading in another language is good for me, though tiring. First, I finish Le Clézio's *Raga*, begun on the beach in Collioure. It's an atmospheric and fascinating book about Oceania. The beauty and strangeness, the sheer 'outdoorness' of it gives a welcome contrast to my closed-in, sometimes bed-bound state. It literally transports me elsewhere.

For the moment I set aside *Le Chevelure de Bérénice* and take up Djemaï's *Gare du Nord*, the book about three immigrants living in Paris. What I would call a very *necessary* book, as well as being a joy to read. It's a reminder of one of the main functions of literature – to allow us, to some (if limited) extent to get inside the lives, the minds, the feelings of people different from ourselves; to develop empathy, and thus kindness, compassion, understanding that goes beyond mere tolerance. To build civilisation.

The Turkish Nobel laureate Orhan Pamuk sees the history of the novel as the history of human liberation. By putting ourselves in another's shoes and using our imagination we can shed our personal identities and set ourselves free. In *How Fiction Works*, James Wood points out that Ian McEwan's *Atonement* is 'explicitly about the dangers of failing to put oneself in someone else's shoes', and that great fictional lawyer, Atticus Finch, in Harper Lee's *To Kill a Mocking-Bird*, tells his young daughter the importance of learning to put on another man's shoes and walk around in them. And George Eliot, in 'The Natural History of German Life', said she thought the greatest benefit we have to gain from all the arts is 'the extension of our sympathies'. Art, she says, is 'a mode of amplifying experience and extending our contact with our fellow man beyond the bounds of our personal lot.' Maryanne Wolf covers similar territory (but takes it a little further) at the beginning of her engrossing study, *Proust and the Squid: The Story and Science of the Reading Brain*, suggesting that the act of reading allows us to step out of our own consciousness into that of another person, age or culture, and that we 'come back' enriched. And it's a way in which we can 'learn both the commonality and the uniqueness of our own thoughts – that we are individuals, but not alone.' Having our boundaries moved and expanded can change who we are and, more importantly, perhaps (especially for children and young people) who we can imagine ourselves being in the future, and how the world might be changed.

It was books that had helped me imagine I could be a dancer, like Anna Pavlova ... that I could be a writer, like Jo March in *Little Women* ... Through books I'd lived in the nineteenth-century – in Russia, France, the USA, as well as Britain. Recently I'd been a Russian *émigré* in Paris, a repressed woman in Tehran, a dedicated bookseller in Kabul, an American Civil War soldier, a writer travelling through the snow in northern Turkey, and was soon to be a *concierge* in Paris ...

Despite much academic theorising, in recent decades, about what the novel does and doesn't do (I have shelves of it), doesn't this remain one of its most vital and immediate functions for most readers? – an embracing of what is different from ourselves, along with a recognition of what is shared (even more important in a globalised and shrinking world).

I suppose one has to admit that reading blogs and Facebook 'conversations' on the internet is another way of getting inside other people's heads. But we're mainly restricted to the thoughts of people blogging in our own language. How many Russian, or Japanese, or Saudi bloggers do most people follow? But the blog and Facebook forms often seem, to me, to encourage a certain tone, to reduce the writer of them (with some notable exceptions) to personalised, unconsidered burblings, partly because of the frequency with which one is expected to blog (people won't bother to go onto the site if they know there are big gaps between fresh material appearing, I'm told) and to Facebook (is that a verb yet? – 'to Face-book'?). The effectiveness of communication through the worked-on text (the consideration of rhythm and sound as part of effective communication – the aesthetics of writing) is generally, though not universally, absent. One has to ask how interesting are the heads that one can get into by reading the blogs and Facebooks of others. Some are. But many are not as interesting as reading a book that has gone through many stages of refinement before it is made available. We need to read things by people very different from ourselves, but not if they are ill-considered or just plain daft. Life is too short, and there can be advantages to having one's reading already filtered through the process of selection involved in publishing, even if a good many worthy things never make it into traditional print forms.

But back to the books I'm reading at the moment: Abdelkader Djemaï's *Gare du Nord*. In France, as well as England, there are increasing numbers of texts by second-generation immigrants (the first often too busy just surviving and raising a family in a foreign and often hostile land), or by those of mixed immigrant and British parentage (like Zadie Smith,

Monica Ali, Hanif Kureishi, and poet Moniza Alvi).
We need to open our minds to their stories – though
I wonder if this particular gem, *Gare du Nord*, will
ever be translated into English.

I'm ready for something longer, more demanding,
and begin *L'Élégance du hérisson* – 'The Elegance of
the Hedgehog'. (Although I first read it in French,
there is now an excellent translation, by Alison
Anderson.)

The 'hedgehog' of the title refers to Renée, a fifty-
four-year-old *concierge*, the main character. The story
is told in the alternating voices of the *concierge* and
a rich but unhappy young girl who lives with her
rather ghastly bourgeois family in the apartment
block serviced by Renée. The wonderful conceit of
the novel is that, while conforming outwardly to the
stereotype of the *concierge* – in her appearance, her
enormous cat, her TV always on in the background,
in her manner of dealing with the residents – Renée
is actually a formidable autodidact, widely read in
literature, history, philosophy, and very knowledge-
able about and appreciative of classical music, art, and
film. (One morning finds her reading Husserl's *Médi-
tations cartésiennes: introduction à la phénoménologie*.)
She's terrified of being 'found out' … which she eventually is when a charming and truly civilised Japanese

gentleman comes to live in the block. Two things alert him to the truth about her: the name of her cat, Leon, after Leo Tolstoy, linking up with the fact that, in conversation, she inadvertently lets slip a well-known quotation from Tolstoy. The Japanese gentleman is both fascinated by Renée and deeply appreciates her. They become close (if unexpected) friends … though not without a good deal of comedy on the way and much encouragement from the concierge's Portuguese *confidante* (the latter ignorant of the intellectual accomplishments of her friend).

The other voice – that of the young girl – is a highly troubled one at the start. Sensitive and intelligent, she is being driven mad by the conduct of her family, especially her flouncing, self-absorbed and rude (especially to Renée) older sister. At the start of the narrative the young girl tells us she has every intention of setting fire to the apartment block and committing suicide. (I won't give away the ending.)

Apart from anything else, the novel provides a delicate and intelligent appreciation of Japanese culture and civility. A superb read.

(And when the ambulance comes for me the next time – another problem with the chemo, though not as bad as the first time – I make sure I push it into my overnight bag, hoping I'll get chance to carry on reading it if I have to stay in again.)

One of the admirable effects of this novel is to remind one that people are usually more complex and interesting than their surfaces suggest. It reminds us of the *surprisingness* of people, but also, sadly, of their often unused capacities. If only we could believe there were an *army* of concierges like Renée. If only they really did watch classic Japanese cinema on the TV screens rather than game shows. Though would it make their lives richer (as Renée's clearly is – and she knows it) or just harder to bear? Is it saying there's no reason why they shouldn't be like Renée, if they wanted to? … just as there's no reason why any of us shouldn't spend our lives more interestingly. It's a novel with a lot of different things to say but, best of all, taken up by the characters and situation, we don't always realise they've been said until we close the book after reading the last page.

Although this time I'm put in a room on my own (to lessen risk of infection – my immune system is 'down'), being back in the hospital makes me think about the people on the ward during my first admission. What were the surprising stories behind their lives? They were very old and clearly not long for this world (I was the only one with bowel control). I couldn't ask them about their stories: it was an effort for them even to give monosyllabic answers to the doctors and nurses. I could only try to imagine their lives from watching their visiting families: mainly not an inspiring experience. All too easy to guess what those ebbing lives had been, when they could have been much more, no doubt. The impatient, irritated way their middle-aged children sometimes talked to them … The often inappropriate, ill-considered gifts … The obvious longing to escape the bedside at the earliest possible moment … Such a sadness it gave me. But still, you never know: maybe little Elsie, who only spoke, with effort, to ask what day or time it was, could hear Bach cello sonatas in her head (or her own equivalent form of beauty or happiness) during her long hours of silence, eyes shut against the ward's fluorescent lights and her own bodily disintegration.

I need a break from reading French – though not a break from France. Amazon has just delivered Graham Robb's *The Discovery of France*, the result of fourteen thousand miles of cycling around the country and lots of research. Utterly, utterly fascinating, and one of those books that changes the way you see and understand a country. And his style makes the reading of the book even more of a pleasure: it's like being in a room with a fascinating, witty and enthusiastic friend, telling you things you'll never forget because they're just *so darned interesting* … like the whistling language (one of France's many extinct languages and dialects – French was once only spoken by a minority of its citizens) used by shepherds in the mountains, a language so sophisticated that they could communicate, over long distances, the contents of an entire newspaper!

It's a long book, but I get a large chunk of it read during my third hospital admission (an infection requiring intravenous antibiotics if I'm not to die of sepsis) – another quiet little room on my own so I can enjoy the book without the continual trauma of other people's illness.

On finishing the book, I'm so reluctant to part from Graham Robb's voice that I immediately romp through his appropriately energetic biography of Balzac (I'd loved his books on Rimbaud and Victor Hugo). We hear him on a New York book programme, thanks to the brilliant facility of internet radio. And like him even more. He sounds just as pleasant, witty, unarrogant and interesting as his books. We say we wish we could be his friend … then we realise that we sort of are. It's a bit of a cliché (it's been doing the rounds for hundreds of years), but one of the great things about books is that their authors can feel like 'friends' – with the advantage of not having to remember their birthdays or feel guilty about not having them to dinner often enough.

Next I read a couple of short novels in translation – *Soldiers of Salamis*, by Javier Cercas, and *Heroes Like Us*, by Thomas Brussig, then go on to Knut Hamsun's famous *Hunger* (which I'm ashamed of not having read before; it was partly the knowledge of his Nazi sympathies that had kept me from it).

Soldiers of Salamis, translated from the Spanish by Anne McLean (it had won the Independent Foreign Fiction prize 2004) turns on an incident in the Spanish Civil War when a fascist writer (who later becomes a national hero), having escaped a firing squad by fleeing into a forest, finds himself looking into the face (and the gun) of one of his Republican pursuers. But instead of killing him, the soldier simply walks away. The story is of the attempt to discover who the compassionate soldier was, why he spared his enemy, and whether he is still alive. Although specifically set in the Spanish Civil War, it moves, like all good fiction, beyond the realms of a specific place and time in what it has to say about human behaviour in general, particularly in the context of war.

Heroes Like Us, translated from the German by John Brownjohn, centres on the fall of the Berlin Wall in 1989. That much I can remember – that and a general 'flavour'. But when trying to write about it I realise most of it has drained away as if my mind's a colander: just a little over-cooked cabbage left at the bottom. Virtually no recollection of the details – though I must have quite enjoyed it or I wouldn't have bothered finishing it. Life's too short to bother with books you're not getting anything out of. And what's more I can't even find the book to refresh my memory. It's not where it should be on my shelves (foreign fiction: German). And it's not even where it shouldn't be. I've scoured every other shelf. I don't remember lending it to anyone. It's as if the book has taken itself off in a huff because I didn't remember it. Though in reality it's probably just dropped behind the piano or down the back of my unshiftably heavy desk … Eventually I think to try under the sofa: success. Several books later, I re-read it quickly, and enjoy it hugely. Maybe I just hadn't been in the mood for its 'Germanic humour', as one reviewer put it. Right and wrong times for some books.

Hunger, translated from the Norwegian by Robert Bly, I find powerful but somehow irritating. It does give an impressive insight into what it's like to have nothing, to be hungry almost to the point of death, to never know where the next penny's coming from, and to have the constant problem of shelter and how to keep warm. It increases one's awareness (or strongly reminds one) of the problems of the deepest underclass in our society. It also shows the desperate protagonist is still able to retain dignity and the ability to carry out kind acts towards others: he is not totally dehumanised by the extremity of his need, and that is his saving grace (because sometimes you feel like shaking him). In fact I am glad to finish it and get onto J. M. Coetzee's *Diary of a Bad Year*, which I like a lot less than his other books. I don't want to say much about it because it might turn into a disproportionate put down of a writer I hugely admire. Am I simply having trouble with fiction? Is it my state of mind? Or is it the books themselves? Three in a row that haven't really fed me in the way I need at the moment.

I have a Doctorow novel – *The March* – from some time back that I haven't read and decide to try: a suitably gruesome and distressing (but very compulsive) story of the American Civil War about which I am really quite ignorant, apart from what I picked up years ago from *Little Women*, from the biography of its author, Louisa May Alcott, and from a brief visit to Gettysburg. But it still doesn't give me the kind of satisfaction I've got from my recent non-fiction reads. Maybe it's a phase. Maybe it's just getting older, or getting more easily irritated by certain fictional tricks that one becomes wise to over the years. Or maybe the fiction itself just isn't … well, that brilliant, or not the kind I need just at the moment. Maybe certain books are right for certain times in one's life and others just aren't.

I pick up another book that's been on my shelf for ages and which I'd started but hadn't then got too far with (we're waiting for the next Amazon delivery – slower than usual with the approach of Christmas): *The World of the Paris Café: Sociability among the French working class, 1789–1914*, by W. Scott Haine. Brilliant. Riveting. Full of fascinating detail and, if you're a lover of Paris cafés, will add a whole new level to your appreciation of them and what they'd stood for, socially and politically, over time. (My daughter gave a copy to a French friend who loved it too, so it's obviously not just for mad English Francophiles.)

Next, a biography. Again a book waiting to be read for a long time (that Amazon order still hasn't come ...). *Flaubert: A Life*, by Geoffrey Wall. I'd read quite a lot about Flaubert when teaching Julian Barnes' *Flaubert's Parrot*, but nothing as sustained and thorough as this book. There's a bookmark a few pages in, so one of us must have started it before. Is it a bad sign, this evidence of rapid abandonment? Is it too badly written to cope with? But there are all sorts of reasons for such abandonments – often the acquisition of something more urgent (or just plain enjoyable) to read. Which must have been the case with this book, which is involving right from the start. It's good to revisit Flaubert … and to reminisce about the visit we'd made to the Rouen hospital where Flaubert's father had been an eminent physician and where little Gustave was brought up. When we visited, part of it had been turned into a rather half-hearted kind of Flaubert museum: you had to ring the bell for entry. We were the only visitors that day and the suitably white-coated *gardien* (was he trying to make himself look like a doctor?) gave us a conducted tour and proudly pointed out the stuffed parrot that featured in Barnes' novel (though whether it was the 'right' parrot we'll never know: see Barnes' novel for the full import of that statement). We enjoyed the pride and modest swagger of the *gardien* as he told us, '*Oui*,' he had come to know '*Monsieur Barnes*' very well.

Why is it that we love to meet writers in the flesh and not just in print? Why do we flock to book festivals? Or get a thrill out of spotting famous writers in unlikely places? I'm as much of a sucker for such things as anyone else. I once actually found myself sitting opposite Julian Barnes in an underground train. Northern Line. Goodge Street. I spent the whole journey studiously not looking at him, though I suspect he'd somehow sensed I'd recognised him and spent the whole journey with his head craned at ninety degrees, looking out of the window ... though as the whole journey was in a tunnel, all he could have been looking at was a point-blank reflection of himself. I once bumped into Doris Lessing in the 'Ladies' at the National Theatre. I must have given her a look of happy recognition because she gave back to me the most luminous smile I have ever received: unforgettable. And I sat just in front of Harold Pinter and Lady Antonia Fraser at some event held in London University. I can't remember the event, but I remember their presence and the lovely way they spoke to each other. Are we interested to compare their writing selves with their 'real world' selves? Or is it just some crass celebrity thing? Or is it because we've been told that writers put the best of themselves into their writing and we want to make sure there's not *too* big a gap between the two? Is it a fear of being taken in? Of some kind of hypocrisy? And can we really know our deeper purposes, anyway?

Where was I? Oh, yes: the Flaubert Museum in Rouen ...

Do such literary pilgrimages help one understand a writer's work better? Sometimes yes, sometimes no. Our visit to Strindberg's claustrophobic house in Stockholm might not have elucidated his plays in any direct way, but there was certainly something about its atmosphere that seemed to underscore certain aspects of their emotional colour, I think. Or were we reading plays into the house? Certainly, when I read the Graham Robb biography I was glad to have visited both Balzac's house near Tours and the one in Paris, simply because I could visualise them when they were mentioned. And I agree with Harold Bloom that a good biography of a novelist can be a useful aid to reading their work, provided we 'avoid the error that good biographers avoid, which is to read the life too closely into the work.' It is 'the work in the writer' that is more important, such as 'the effect of Proust's ambitious project upon the author's own life', as Harold Bloom puts it, in *How to Read and Why*.

At last! The Amazon order!

More biographies. *The End of Youth: the life and work of Alain-Fournier*, by Robert Gibson; *Leonard Woolf: A Life*, by Victoria Glendinning; *The Owl of Minerva: a memoir*, by Mary Midgely; and *Passionate Minds: the great scientific affair* – between Voltaire and Émilie du Châtelet – by David Bodanis, plus three non-biographies on some of my favourite subjects, *Modernism: the lure of heresy*, by Peter Gay, *Musicophilia: stories of music and the brain*, by Oliver Sacks, and *How to Read Montaigne*, by Terence Cave.

I'm not sure how I feel about the Alain-Fournier biography, though it's well-written and interesting. The one book he's known for (he died a premature death in the First World War), *Le Grand Meaulnes*, is strange, elusive, much loved and much taught to young people. It hovers between the real and the unreal, enchanting the reader equally with sharply-observed naturalistic detail and passages of dream-like phantasmagoria. Robert Gibson meticulously traces the book's possible origins in the places, personalities, and relationships of Alain-Fournier's actual life. It's a wonderful piece of research as well as an act of considerable imaginative identification with a writer's mind, but by pulling the novel so completely down to earth, as it were, rather destroys some element of its magic. I'll never be able to read it in quite the same way again. Something of the mystery has gone.

And I suppose this is one of the risks when you open a book – open yourself to what a book has to tell you: it may have a negative effect. I found myself becoming very irritated by Alain-Fournier himself, too. Sometimes I wanted to shake him! But one mustn't let the personality of the author determine one's response to their work – which is usually a distillation of the best of themselves. (It probably wouldn't have been a bundle of fun to live with Flaubert … or Tolstoy …). Even the best novels aren't written by saints but by erring humans with, we hope, compassionate and attentive minds.

I already know quite a lot about Leonard Woolf through biographies of Virginia Woolf and books on 'Bloomsbury' in general. But Victoria Glendinning's biography reveals a depth, complexity, energy, talent and commitment only hinted at elsewhere. An additional interest is the insight into British Colonialism (Woolf was for a time a colonial administrator in Ceylon writing a highly regarded novel based on his experiences there, *The Village in the Jungle*), as well as into other political aspects of the period in which he was deeply involved. He just worked *so hard* for what he believed in, and had Virginia's severe mental health problems to deal with, too – not to mention the general shenanigans of her friends and family, with whom he wasn't altogether in tune. He also found time to do the gardening.

I finish the book with a huge respect for the man, but a kind of sadness that, despite all his hard work, at the end of a long life he still felt he hadn't managed to make as much of an *obvious* difference to the world as he would have liked – which probably goes for most of us.

Moral philosopher Mary Midgley's memoir, *The Owl of Minerva*, is the next thing I read. A charming, insightful account of a happy, intelligent, compassionate, mainly privileged life spent in worthwhile endeavours. And early in the book I enjoy one of those sudden moments of connection – one of those threads joining one to another's life and experience – when Midgley mentions her move from being a fiction addict since childhood to preferring non-fiction, adding that most of her friends have had the same experience. So, are my recent dissatisfactions with fiction age related? A moment of reassurance, of recognition. One of the pleasures of reading: solidarity. (It can't *all* be challenge and new places: too exhausting!)

Inside the back cover of *The Owl of Minerva* I make a note to read Boethius' *Consolations of Philosophy*, which Midgley refers to. It's one of those texts one might know from references in other texts, and I didn't know, until reading Midgley (or had forgotten) that he'd written it while in prison awaiting execution. I think it's true to say that most cancer patients – no matter how treatable the form they have of the disease, no matter how good the prognosis – feel as if they've been given a capital sentence, without knowing, usually, for how long they'll be on death row or how effective the appeals will be. So suddenly a fine, unexpected thread is thrown across the centuries from

Boethius to me. By thinking, Mary Midgley writes, he managed to achieve a state of mind that was not only courageous but deeply friendly and benign. He was able to offer genuine comfort to others. (I don't think I can go that far … but yes, I should read Boethius. Though not yet.)

From the 'passionate mind' of Mary Midgley, I go to *Passionate Minds* – David Bodanis's portrait of the relationship between Enlightenment philosopher and writer Voltaire and the great scientific mind and ardent body of Émilie du Châtelet. I've already read a couple of books covering some of the same eighteenth-century territory of that fascinating, modern-world-shaping period (including Roger Pearson's *Voltaire Almighty: a life in pursuit of freedom*, and Philipp Blom's *Encyclopédie: the triumph of reason in an unreasonable age* – both very, very good and enjoyable), but the pleasures of Bodanis's account include the greater weight given to de Châtelet's achievements, which, like so many of women's contributions to traditional male spheres, have been down-played in (if not entirely written out of) the standard histories.

Voltaire himself comes across as sometimes petulant and often irritating, with his hypochondria and unnecessary risk-taking, avoiding arrest for anti-monarchism by the skin of his teeth and no stranger to the inside of the Bastille. During their affair, he not only greatly encouraged Émilie's scientific work but tried to be a scientist himself. She, however, had the lightning-quick mind of a mathematical genius and the ability to see to the heart of scientific problems way beyond Voltaire's capacities, and in the end he had to admit defeat and return to literature.

I already knew the tragic end of the story. Voltaire and Émilie remained close friends even after their physical intimacy was over, but during the fag-end of her affair with a careless younger man, she became pregnant, at the age of forty-two. She knew it was a virtual death sentence. Full of sadness at her life being cut short in this trivially accidental way and racing against her own biology, she worked tirelessly to complete her great scientific project before the inevitable departure. She died of infection a week after giving birth. Her baby (a girl) also died.

If she'd lived as long as me, what else might she have achieved?

Her translation into French of Newton's *Principia* and her brilliant explication of it was fundamental to key developments in theoretical physics in the eighteenth century and helped to lay the groundwork for a great deal of contemporary science. She was also important in the general spread of Enlightenment ideas, showing particular kindness and support to the encyclopædist Denis Diderot (one of my personal heroes). Even when eight months pregnant and hurrying to finish her project before the birth, she took time out to use family connections to make sure that Diderot, then imprisoned on account of his Enlightenment beliefs, was well treated. In his eulogy, Voltaire wrote: '*Her memory is treasured by all who knew her intimately, and who were capable of perceiving the breadth of her mind.*' It's a great service to bring such a woman to wider attention through such a lively and readable account of her life and its historical and scientific context. Admirable, admirable book in every way …

Oliver Sacks' *Musicophilia* describes the functioning of the human brain in relation to music. Just as Freud developed his theories largely through the observation of damaged minds, so in Sacks' study the way that music emerges from and acts upon the human brain comes to light first in relationship to the abnormal – extreme instances of brain damage, for example, provoking sudden musical talent. From such examples it is possible to investigate the more general human capacities for performing and responding to those patterns of sound-waves acting upon our eardrums and which we call 'music'. And, as always, Oliver Sacks' style makes the study an utter pleasure to read. Another writer, like Graham Robb, whose books make you feel you're in a room having a conversation with a well-informed but humorous friend.

'Modernism' – in literature, art, and music – has always been my home territory. In an odd sort of way I see it as a natural development from, or adjunct to, an interest in the Enlightenment. Though I've already got lots of books on Modernism, I can't resist any new ones that appear, and my investment in the hardback of Peter Gay's *Modernism: the lure of heresy – from Baudelaire to Beckett and beyond* proves worth the money. Although covering some familiar ground, it's also full of fresh insights and connections. Already I want to go back and read the whole book again.

Why is it we feel more at home in some periods than in others? Why can't I feel the same enthusiasm for the Victorians, say, as for the Modernists? What do I get out of the latter that I don't get out of the former?

Rebellion. That's one possible answer.

Despite appearances to the contrary, I'm a rebel – and something of a bohemian, at least in the domestic sphere ...'Excuse my dust': it leaves more time for reading.

∽ FIVE ∾

'Why don't you use the library, like I do?'

My mother is visiting when yet another Amazon delivery arrives. Does the amount I'm spending on books bother her?

How to explain?

There are obvious things like, 'they don't have the books I want to read', and even if they were order-able I don't want to have to wait weeks for someone else to finish with a book, remember (eventually) to return it, wait for its transfer to our local library and for them to inform me etc etc. I WANT IT NOW! And I don't want to have to remember to keep renewing it, nor to take it back too soon if someone else orders it. And you can't mark library books. You can't make those important notes in the margin or underline bits or fill in the blank spaces with notes. (But I tell my mother it's because of the 'germs': she understands about my immune system being poor at the moment.)

And you have to give library books back. In her extended essay on Antigua, *A Small Place*, Jamaica Kincaid tells how once she'd read a book she couldn't bear to part with it and even stole books from her childhood library as a result of this impulse to own what she had read. In *A Reading Diary*, Alberto Manguel also says that reading a book and knowing he doesn't own it gives him the feeling of something incomplete, only half enjoyed. I know how they feel. If you don't have in your possession the books you've read, they won't be catching your eye as you pass them on your shelf, reminding you of the experience of reading them, where you were in your life at the time, what it felt like to be taken to the particular place that particular book took you to. They won't be the voice of a friend calling 'hello' each time your eye snags on the spine. I admit to suffering from bibliokleptomania. Alberto Manguel writes of his love of possessing books as 'a sort of voluptuous greed'. I share his enjoyment of crowded bookshelves and his delight in being surrounded by what amounts to an inventory of one's life. There's also the joy of coming across bits and pieces stashed away in the books – old tickets, notes, scraps of paper – that conjure up places, times, people, events attached to when the book was acquired or read. Books can help remind us of the richness of the life we've led.

This is quite a different impulse from wanting to own books 'for show', even though owning them is inevitably part of the identity one constructs for oneself through whatever one owns, or chooses not to own.

When I go to a house for the first time, I head for the bookshelves as soon as I decently can. We have several close friends whose libraries overlap significantly with our own: we've sprung from shared soil so understand each other, feel at ease in each other's company. But it's always interesting to check out what we don't share, to get further ideas for reading from people whose preferences you trust. I can, however, imagine going to a house where the 'visible' bookshelves are suspiciously more interesting than their owners; I'd probably wonder if the books on them had been selected to create a particular impression on visitors. (Perhaps we all do that to some extent – my mother always did more housework when visitors were due.) I think I'd be especially sceptical if they were neat and didn't have volumes thrust in horizontally and at random. We are what we read – not just what we appear to read. One would quickly smell a biblio-rat.

But getting back to the subject of public libraries: I don't want to give the impression that I under-value them, just because I'm lucky enough to own most of the books I read. With continual threats to the very existence of many of them, I want to champion the immeasurable value – and the distinguished and fascinating histories – of the world's libraries. They are the under-pinning of civilisation.

The Papal library at Avignon was, before the invention of printing, the only one in Western Europe to contain more than two thousand volumes. Modern print technology means I can fit a tenth of these into three small shelves among the dozens our personal library occupies (while microchip technology, of course, allows thousands of books to be carried in a pocket). I've never counted how many books we have, but I know we can't equal the great library of Alexandria, which surely haunts the dreams of all bibliophiles. It's mentioned in just about every book on books and reading I've ever come across. And at the expense of risking repetition, I'm going to give the basic facts here. (Skip the next paragraph if you already know the story.)

It was Ptolemy the First who, in the third century BCE, founded the great library that was to make Alexandria so famous. It came to house nearly half a million scrolls, plus another forty thousand stored in a separate overflow building. The aim was for the library to contain the whole of human knowledge. One method of expanding the collection was to demand that any ship stopping at Alexandria render up all books on board for copying, after which they – or the copies – would be returned. (Such scrolls were identified by having the words *from the ships* stamped on them.) The library as total global brain. The modern equivalent is the 'deposit library', to which all publishers are required to send a copy of every single book published. (The British Library in London is the most well-known of these deposit libraries in the UK, but there are several others.)

The library of Alexandria was destroyed by fire around 640 CE: a bibliophile's nightmare. In *The Yellow-Lighted Bookshop*, Lewis Buzbee fleshes out the story. When Muslim armies conquered the city, there was a debate about the worth of the library. Caliph Omar's representative, Ibn Amrou el-Ass, was swayed by the arguments of the librarian John Philoponus that, as the library's contents pre-dated the Prophet, they were not 'infidel' texts, and many of the greatest works were of Arabic origin. But the fundamentalist Caliph Omar was not swayed, asserting that the Koran was the only book anyone needed and ordered the contents of the library to be distributed around the bath-houses of Alexandria and burnt to heat the water. It took six months for them all to be consumed by flames.

Today, however, there is a vast new library in Alexandria (it was begun in 1988) with enough shelf-space for over 8,000,000 books, besides audio-visual and virtual forms of knowledge. The first chapter of Alberto Manguel's *The Library at Night* includes a very good section on the old Alexandria library, plus an aerial photo of the new one.

Alexandria wasn't the only ancient library (though it's the most famous). Other great institutions include the library at Thebes: the inscription over its entrance, 'Medicine for the Soul', suggests that the therapeutic aspects of reading – bibliotherapy – have long been officially recognised. The library of Ashurbanipal, at Nineveh, was founded between 669 and 631 BCE, while in China records show there was an imperial library at the time of the Qin dynasty (around the third century BCE), if not before. And a library curator of the Han dynasty (second to first century BCE) is thought to have set up China's first classification system.

Persia had many libraries, including the royal library of Isfahan and an important public library at Gunishapur dating from 667 CE. Christian and Islamic libraries flourished in the Middle Ages and included the great Sufiya library in Aleppo, attached to the Grand Umayyad Mosque. Many other mosques also sponsored public libraries which, as 'halls of science', were quite widespread by the ninth century, covering secular as well as religious knowledge. Tenth-century Shiraz had a huge library in an attractive setting of gardens, lakes and waterways.

The material qualities and setting of a library – whether a great national institution or a room in school – can make a great deal of difference to its users. One of our local libraries, built into an office complex and replacing a charming nineteenth century building (now occupied by a nursery school) has no windows. The claustrophobia of this plus the effects of the fluorescent lights makes it one of the last places I would want to sit and read. Another local library – smaller and with less stock – has large windows on two sides, creating a much more inviting atmosphere, even though the views are not particularly glamorous. A small car park on one side, but a patch of grass, a tree that blossoms lusciously in spring and a flower-bed on the other, and the shops and traffic beyond. Books as part of life, not hermetically sealed in a stifling little world of their own. (How awful to work in that windowless library!)

How much better to take as a model for our libraries the second-century library of Hadrian in the Roman Agora in Athens. As well as a magnificent cloistered courtyard (bordered by a hundred columns) around a pool, it also housed music rooms, lecture rooms, and a theatre. A rather bleak modern equivalent is Paris's Bibliothèque François Mitterand, the shape of four open books (at a stretch of the imagination) around a central space that contains a small square of forest. And the new British Library? It's 'all right', but there's still something missing. Perhaps white marble against a blue sky would … Oh, well.

Because the great majority of writers are, almost by definition, readers and book-lovers, libraries and bookshops often find their way into writing.

In Boris Pasternak's *Doctor Zhivago*, it's in a library that Yuri meets up once more with Larissa Antipova ('Lara') – a chance meeting that launches the affair they'd carefully avoided during their earlier period of working together as doctor and nurse. The description of the library and its users might seem a little more detailed than strictly necessary to establish it as the site of the encounter (he doesn't even speak to her there: only discovers her address after she leaves just as he decides to approach her). To me there seems a sense of the writer's pleasure in creating the library so vividly for the reader … and maybe for himself.

It's in Bouville ('Mud-town') library that Roquentin, the narrator of Jean-Paul Sartre's *Nausea* makes the acquaintance of the Autodidact, doggedly reading his way through the public library in alphabetical order – which elicits a scathing response from Roquentin/Sartre. (In fact, the Autodidact comes off very badly altogether in the novel: unattractive as he is, I've always felt a little sorry for him.)

But one of the most enjoyable library depictions has to be in Virginia Woolf's *Jacob's Room*: a portrait of the old Reading Room in the British Museum, still totally recognisable – right down to the presence of various eccentrics – when I briefly used it before the new British Library became operational and the old Reading Room was opened to the public first as an exhibit (partly the cult of celebrity? – all the famous people who'd read and written there) and later as an exhibition space. I imagine Woolf had great fun writing this:

Not so very long ago the workmen had gilt the final 'y' in Lord Macaulay's name, and the names stretched in unbroken file round the dome of the British Museum. At a considerable depth beneath, many hundreds of the living sat at the spokes of a cart-wheel copying from printed books into manuscript books; now and then rising to consult the catalogue; regaining their places stealthily while from time to time a silent man replenished their compartments.

There was a little catastrophe. Miss Marchmont's pile overbalanced and fell into Jacob's compartment. Such things happened to Miss Marchmont. What was she seeking through millions of pages, in her old plush dress, and her wig of claret-coloured hair, with her gems and her chilblains? Sometimes one thing, sometimes another, to confirm her philosophy that colour is sound – or, perhaps, it has something to do with music. She could never quite say, though it was not for lack of trying […] But she needed funds to publish her book, for 'publishers are capitalists – publishers are cowards.' And so, digging her elbow into her pile of books it fell over.

Jacob remained quite unmoved.

But Fraser, the atheist, on the other side, detesting plush, more than once accosted with leaflets, shifted irritably [...]

Miss Julia Hedge, the feminist, waited for her books. They did not come. She wetted her pen. She looked about her. Her eye was caught by the final letters in Lord Macaulay's name. And she read them all round the dome – the names of the great men which remind us – 'Oh damn,' said Julia Hedge, 'why didn't they leave room for an Eliot or a Brontë?' Unfortunate Julia! Wetting her pen in bitterness, and leaving her shoelaces untied. When her books came she applied herself to her gigantic labours, but perceived through one of the nerves of her exasperated sensibility how composedly, unconcernedly, and with every consideration the male readers applied themselves to theirs. That young man, for example. What had he got to do except copy out poetry?

[...] The books were now replaced. A few letters of the alphabet were sprinkled around the dome. Closely stood together in a ring round the dome were Plato, Aristotle, Sophocles, and Shakespeare; the literatures of Rome, Greece, China, India, Persia. One leaf of poetry was pressed flat against another, one burnished letter

laid smooth against another in a density of meaning, a conglomeration of loveliness.

[...] There is in the British Museum an enormous mind. Consider that Plato is there cheek by jowl with Aristotle: and Shakespeare with Marlowe. This great mind is hoarded beyond the power of any single mind to possess it.

But there are sinister libraries, too. In his bleak short story, 'The Library of Babel', Borges chooses to represent the Universe as a frightening and puzzling library composed of an infinite number of hexagonal galleries. An echo of this is found in the abbey library of Umberto Eco's *The Name of the Rose* with its heptagonal chambers. The library is linked to a series of murders and ends up in flames, as does the personal library of Professor Peter Kien, the protagonist of Elias Canetti's *Auto da Fé*. But such fictional conflagrations cannot compete with the real thing: Sultan Khan of Åsne Seierstad's *The Bookseller of Kabul* (translated by Ingrid Christophersen) had to watch piles of his books being publicly burnt by illiterate soldiers. As 'a free-thinker and of the opinion that everyone had the right to be heard', he had long braved the Taliban authorities in order to keep the people of Kabul supplied with the nourishment of books. On his way to detention he consoled himself with the knowledge that the most prohibited books were ingeniously hidden, stashed away behind the counter: the 'armed half-wits' hadn't thought to look there.

The burning of books: the bibliophile's nightmare, whether carried out by Nazis, religious extremists, or simple philistines. Each burning an echo of the great library of Alexandria ... though the exiled Russian poet, Joseph Brodsky, suggested that a worse crime than burning books is not to read them.

The worst library destruction I've heard of – and which has haunted me ever since I first read of it in Alberto Manguel's *A History of Reading* – was the one that took place in Sachsenhausen concentration camp. It was the murder of a famous scholar who, having during his life memorised many of the classics, offered himself as a 'living library' to his fellow prisoners. In the absence of actual books, they could make requests and the scholar would recite the texts for them. Books against barbarity. Manguel adds that the murdered scholar was immortalised in Ray Bradbury's novel about book destruction, *Fahrenheit 451°*, as one of the roaming 'book-savers'.

Libraries rise and fall, are opened, are closed, become sites of memory. The new British Library replaces the old British Library whose Reading Room – once an exclusive club for scholars and eccentrics – is opened to the public. That's good. That's very good. But when I visited after the big changes at the British Museum (but before the library was turned into an exhibition space), I felt a weird kind of guilt at just walking in without showing my obtained-with-a-lot-of-effort pass and without being scrutinised by the ever-suspicious guards for possible evil intents towards books.

I was once nearly banned from using the British Library for having inadvertently conveyed some book or document to *the wrong part of the Reading Room*, thus contravening some rule I was unaware of. The response of the two librarians when my fault was discovered seemed so ludicrously threatening that I began to wonder if they were after a bribe to prevent me from being 'struck off'. But this was England, this was 'The British Library'. With my gibbering innocence finally accepted, I gave grovelling thanks and promised never, *ever* to do it again.

Over-zealous? Or just bad-tempered? – like the librarian who used to get cross with Malcolm, when he was a little boy, for 'reading the books too quickly'. Those stamped out on a Saturday morning he would sometimes return, read, in the afternoon. Though regularly told off for this (maybe it interfered with some 'system'), it didn't – happily – put him off reading as it might have done a more timid child. And maybe his love of going to the library was even connected to his obvious power to annoy a grown up, an authority figure. An original form of rebellion?

Surely one of the best-loved libraries ever was forced to close in 2005, much to the dismay of many people. The old Whitechapel Library, in London's East End – the 'university of the ghetto' as it was known – became history at 5 p.m. on Saturday 6th August, 2005. Founded in 1892 by the Liberal MP J. Passmore Edwards, the beautiful building he paid for (believing only the best was good enough for 'the common people') straddled the entrance to Aldgate East underground station and adjoined the Whitechapel Art Gallery (another Passmore Edwards project). This has now taken over the old library building: a radical renovation has provided the gallery with much needed additional display space and extra facilities. The brand new 'Whitechapel Ideas Store', with state-of-the-art technology, 'learning spaces', crèche, etc, replaces the old library ... which, however, has a happy after-life in the memories of so many people whose lives it changed through making books available when they were not in a position to buy them. Apart from the nameless thousands of beneficiaries, the library helped to educate such well-known people as Jacob Brownowski (the scientist and historian famous for this TV series, *The Ascent of Man*), poet Isaac Rosenberg (1890–1918), artists Mark Gertler (1891–1939) and David Bomberg (1890–1957), authors Simon Blumenfeld (1907–2005) and Willy Goldman (b.1910), and playwrights Arnold Wesker (b.1932) and Bernard Kops (b.1926). (A poem by Bernard Kops summing up just what the Whitechapel Library had meant to people like himself can be easily found on the web.)

I only visited the Whitechapel Library once – shortly before its closure – even though it was just along the road from where I was an undergraduate. We had a magnificent college library so I never needed to use it. The library of Queen Mary College (in the Mile End Road) was a kind of mini version of the old British Library's Reading Room. I imagine it has since been modernised. Originally it was part of the old 'People's Palace', an institution founded, like the Whitechapel Library, to provide the deprived people of East London with free access to books, education, music, theatre, opportunities.

We should celebrate our specialist libraries, too. The ever-expanding Poetry Library on London's South Bank houses, besides the most amazing collection of poetry books, a vast accumulation of literary magazines and journals. The library as archive. Even some of the most obscure and transitory literary magazines can be found there. Many such libraries have fascinating and inspiring histories – like the Women's Library, originating from the London National Society for Women's Suffrage, an organisation established in 1867. It was originally housed in a former public house in Marsham Street, Westminster, becoming, in the 1930s, a major women's centre just a short walk from Parliament. Among its members were politicians and writers – including Virginia Woolf who, in a letter to the composer Dame Ethel Smyth, wrote: 'I think it is almost the only satisfactory deposit for stray guineas'. The library is now held under the auspices of the LSE, which stepped in when its previous university home could no longer accommodate it and the precious collection was in danger of being broken up.

The prospect of a preciously acquired collection of books being broken up or discarded is distressing to the true bibliophile. In her *Ex Libris: Confessions of a Common Reader*, the American writer and journalist Anne Fadiman describes how, after five years of marriage, she and her husband finally combine their books. When Malcolm and I did the same thing (though I can't remember how long we'd been living together when we undertook the operation), we recognised it was a firmer commitment to each other than any wedding ceremony could ever be. Once blended, it would probably have been much harder and more time-consuming to disentangle our personal libraries than for the legally wedded to get a divorce.

We each have our strengths: he's stronger on the nineteenth-century novel and American literature, but I have all the Anglo-Saxon and Mediæval stuff. He is big on politics and history, and I have more philosophy – though we each have the same Penguin edition of Plato's *Republic*. And there's a good deal of overlap and repetition: the plays of Molière, Maupassant's short stories, two copies of Stendhal's *Scarlet and Black*, and no less than four of *Madame Bovary*. Then there's T. S. Eliot, Sylvia Plath, Robert Frost, Anna Akhmatova …

Anne Fadiman describes how she and her husband reached decisions, in the case of 'double copies', about whose copy to discard. But there was never any question, with us, of ditching *any* of them! – not because we thought we'd ever unravel the library and go our separate ways, nor because we had a generous amount of space in which to house them, but because we both loved *the actual books* we'd read, studied, made notes on, had our names in. Not book as 'fetish', though; book as valued companion. Embarrassing, yes, some of those 'very trues' and exclamation marks in the margins of our youth, along with those terribly meaningful underlinings, but it's how we were *then*, discovering the world of books and the world *through* books. (It led us to each other.) Portraits of our younger selves that we could smile at but shouldn't denigrate or discard. Books as snapshots of oneself at a particular age or stage (long hair, bell-bottoms and all).

And now for the story of Mr W ...

During my time as a teacher, I used to oversee what must be one of the most beautiful secondary-school libraries in the country – a library I'd seen being built while a pupil at the same school, as a fitting memorial to its visionary founder. At either end of its two-storeyed height (the upper portion was a balcony) huge floor-to-ceiling windows gave the loveliest views over trees, green slopes, an orchard, a lake, and London in the distance (on a clear day!). Parents would gasp at the library. Most of the pupils loved it. The staff appreciated it.

The library's fame must have spread to the pupils' families – to some of them, at least – as one day I receive a message that a Mr W., grandfather of one of my pupils, would like me to phone him. It's urgent.

He sounds frail, a little strange, but very determined. He has a great number of books, he says, which he is donating to our library. (There's no 'wished to donate' or 'would we like them'.) He used to be a teacher of English literature and the books will therefore be very useful to us. I must collect them before the end of the week. (It's already Wednesday.) When I tell the librarian, she's sceptical. But Mr W's blind insistence wins the day.

As I don't drive, the librarian agrees to take me. Mr W. lives less than a mile from the school, so at four o'clock on the Friday afternoon, after a day's teaching, I ring the doorbell, holding the two large empty boxes he's commanded me to bring. (The librarian doesn't come in. She'll sit in the car and have a snooze, she says, and reminds me firmly not to be too long. Am I being punished for giving in to Mr W.?)

Thin, stooped, spectacles, a little fine white hair, trembling, and with the beginnings of a confused look that might be the onset of dementia … or simply a sign of emotion.

'Good … good … the extra boxes.' In the corner of his small living-room are about a dozen cardboard boxes already packed with books. (Oh dear. I hadn't realised mine would be 'extra' boxes!) Everything smells of stale cigarette smoke. He insists on making me a cup of tea. While he's in the kitchen, I open the flaps of the three accessible boxes, and flip open one or two covers – and my heart sinks. The librarian, it seems, was right.

Over tea, he explains, with scarcely contained grief and anger, that he's being made to go and live with his daughter who has forbidden him to take with him all but fifty of his life-time's collection of books. 'She doesn't understand what they mean to me.' He trembles as he opens a small blue volume of narrative poems. 'I've already got rid of some of the less precious ones – to charity shops and friends – but the rest ... I want them to go somewhere safe, where they'll be looked after and appreciated and read. I don't want them just thrown out ... or burnt. That's what *she*'d do if I tried to take more than fifty. Burn them. And it's a terrible thing, burning books.' His lips tremble. 'My granddaughter's not much of a reader' – yes, I knew that – 'She takes after her mother. But she talks about the school library and how nice it is there. And some of your youngsters must like books. I'd like to think these ...' (he points to the stacked boxes) 'would be ... loved by someone.'

I think of the titles on the top layers of those boxes I'd peeped into: *A Treatise on the Novel* (*Ex libris* J.W.—, 1947), a biography of Lady Hester Stanhope, Oscar Wilde's *De Profundis*, Edith Sitwell's biography of Alexander Pope, Robert Louis Stevenson's *Virginibus Puerisque* essays ... And I try to make the unlikely picture of our pupils – or even the staff – reading them.

Beside his armchair are precarious towers of books, the ones destined for my two boxes ... which I suggest we start filling as 'time is getting on' and the librarian and I have to deliver the books back to school before going home: we have families to feed.

With some difficulty he manoeuvres himself out of his chair and swivels unsteadily to face the uneven towers. But, in trying to pick up two or three books at the same time, he knocks all the piles into a collapsed Babel ... and can't bend far enough to retrieve a single volume, and certainly not those that have slid under the armchair and under the cupboard in the corner.

'Let's put the first box on the armchair and I'll hand the books to you one at a time: you can pack them,' I suggest.

On hands and knees, grovelling among the avalanches of smoky books on a carpet that gives off a whiff of damp and mould, I begin to hand him the books, one by one ...

Not such a good idea. He turns each book longingly, regretfully, in unsteady hands. 'Oh dear ... I'm not sure. This one? ... I'd really like to ... Oh, I don't know ...' Sometimes he opens them, looks at an inscription. 'I don't really want to part with ...'

It's impossible to hurry him. And what might have become intense irritation on my part is neutralised

– no, much more than neutralised: utterly over-whelmed – by an intense, eye-watering pity for this old man's profound sorrow at being made to part with what had meant so much to him … being made to part with his books at the very time when he needed all the comfort they might be able to offer. (Couldn't his daughter let him keep them in boxes in his bedroom?! Is it really the 'space' she doesn't have? Or is it the smoky smell she doesn't want in the house? – in which case she'll have to burn all his clothes as well. Or is she punishing him for some-thing? For the exhaustion and inconvenience of having to look after him, day and night, in her own house?)

By the time the two 'extra' boxes are packed and the disgruntled librarian has helped me load all the boxes into her boot and onto the back seat (with considerable risk to our spines), it's too late to take them to school: it'll be locked up. The care-taker finishes at five on Fridays. 'I'm not having that smell in *my* house,' grouses the librarian, fed up with the long wait. Which is why they end up in mine. Malcolm and the kids help me move them to the summer house.

A number of the books did, for a time, end up in the school library. (To my knowledge, none was ever read – the librarian was absolutely right to question their usefulness – and soon after I left the school, I came across some of them in a local second-hand bookshop.) But a good number of them have remained in my possession – though relegated to the summer house bookshelves. I don't think Mr W. would mind: they are probably 'loved' – or at least appreciated – more in my library than in the school's. True, I won't read most of them, but I'll treasure them from a sense of fellow-feeling for another bibliophile, another bibliokleptomaniac.

(What will happen to *my* books?)

~ SIX ~

Nearly Christmas. Nine weeks of treatment and I'm getting fed up with the continual tablets and blood tests and hospital visits and feeling lousy and the fear of more dashes to A&E if things go wrong again. Fed up with the nasty familiarity of it all. I try hard not to feel petulant and childish. Most of the time I keep control in front of other people who are relieved to find me 'so cheerful' when they visit. Sometimes I'm acting, sometimes I'm not. Sometimes I do feel okay. But now we've come to the shortest days, the longest nights – nights that the necessary steroids ensure are wakeful for me.

I need some snow.

I've been thinking about snow and why I love it so much – why I always long for it even though one shouldn't because it makes life difficult and dangerous. It interrupts things. I don't care. I want it to snow (though I know it probably won't).

In twentieth-century literary theory – and specifically in the 1917 essay, 'Art as Device' (sometimes translated as 'Art as Technique'), by the Russian Victor Shklovsky – one finds the concept of '*ostranenie*', of 'making strange' or 'defamiliarisation' as it's usually translated (clumsy compared with that lovely word *ostranenie*) as central to all art. The habitual nature of our everyday experiences, he says, makes our perceptions stale and automatic. The purpose of art is to help us recover the sensation of life, to make us *feel* things by means of making objects and sensations unfamiliar. And this, of course, is exactly what snow does. The scruffy garden is turned into a dreamscape, a sparkling wonderland. The tedious, ugly houses opposite (unless you live somewhere like Hampstead or Primrose Hill) are suddenly beautified. Dark and cloddy winter fields turn dazzling, smooth, breathtaking. Pompous civic statues are turned comic with crazy little white hats. And the last straggle of improbable December roses are weighed down with whiteness in an odd juxtaposition of summer and winter.

The defamiliarising effect of snow can make us notice life more acutely – which, according to James Wood, in *How Fiction Works*, is exactly what literature does: it makes us 'better noticers of life,' he says, giving us more to bring to life … which makes us better readers of literature … which makes us better readers of life, etc.

For me, any art worthy of the name – whether writing, painting, photography, music, theatre or dance – should be like snow, the snow of *ostranenie*, transforming the way things appear to us, changing our view, even if minutely. In one of his letters, Kafka expressed the opinion that if a book doesn't 'wake us up with a blow to the head', there's no point reading it. Marilyn French's seventies' novel, *The Women's Room*, carried the strap line '*This book will change your life*', which seems an hubristic claim … until one reflects that any book worth reading is likely to do the same, even if not in a melodramatic way. It will, at least, modify one's view of things, effect small (sometimes perhaps scarcely discernible) changes in the way we see the world and others and, cumulatively, 'change one's life' by changing or extending perceptions. Though sometimes a single book can make a huge change.

I remember a summer holiday which my daughter, thirteen or fourteen at the time, spent mainly up a climbable tree in the garden of the house we'd rented, with a cushion, an umbrella (just in case) and a copy of Harper Lee's *To Kill a Mockingbird*. Towards the end of the holiday, having finished the book, she came down from the tree and announced she would have a career in Law. The character of Atticus Finch and his fight against blatant injustice and prejudice had inspired her – had 'changed her life' (or, at least, given it direction). Today she works in the field of international Human Rights law.

Another holiday – a much earlier one. A lot of rain. Two small children cooped up in the holiday flat. Older brother being, most unusually, a 'pain'. Me, at the end of my maternal tether, hauling him to an armchair, thrusting a book in his hands and saying, 'Sit there. Don't move. Read that' – then thinking to myself, 'Oh my God, what a stupid thing to do!' He was already a rather 'reluctant reader' (as they're labelled in education) and a sure-fire way to put him off completely was to make it a *punishment*. How could I have been so stupid! But the book was C. S. Lewis' *The Lion, the Witch and the Wardrobe* and he was hooked. He demanded the rest of the series immediately and spent the rest of the holiday far away from us and the rain, in the kingdom of Narnia. He hasn't stopped reading since. (He's now a writer, an editor, a reviewer of books.) Right book at the right time (even if for the wrong reason). Books changing lives.

Reading as a transformation of the self. Reading as the builder of an identity that encompasses what is initially outside the self, bringing it into the little room of one's own head. Even making our own life 'strange' to us, learning to see it through others' eyes. The more different the better. Necessary snow.

One example from my recent experience: Robin Bray's translation from the Arabic of Saudi writer Turki al-Hamad's *Adama*. It allows the reader into a world we encounter, for the most part, only fleetingly and most often negatively, through the media. It changes, modifies our view of the country and makes us feel the 'reality' of the people who live there. Despite showing us its many differences from our own society, it also makes us feel our *commonality*: the protagonist is the familiar Romantic figure of the thinking, sensitive young man who feels himself an outsider, at odds with the social groupings and value systems of his country and his generation, questing and questioning like the hero of a hundred European novels. Despite being banned in several countries (with *fatwas* against the author), *Adama* became a best-seller in the Middle East. It's the first of a trilogy (*Shumaisi* and *Karadib* are the second and third).

Then you start wondering about all the worthwhile books that don't get translated, all the riches we're missing out on. How many are we missing out on in Croatian, Spanish, Greek, Estonian, Turkish, Italian, Dutch, Swedish? ... not to mention all the different Chinese, African, and Indian and Far Eastern languages (Japanese, Vietnamese, the languages of the Philippines – like the strange and lovely music of Tagalog that the Filipina nurses speak to each other as they work or exchange information about patients). Though I suppose that in one short life we wouldn't have time to read them all. But it would be nice to know they were available if we wanted to. Some people would read some of them, at least. It might make a difference. It might change the world, gradually, very gradually. (Be optimistic or die.)

An article I read a while ago stated that less than 3% of books published in the USA are translations from other languages (which says a lot, though one doesn't like to mention cultural isolation and arrogance; or is it the fear of having to modify entrenched perceptions of the world? ... a kind of complacent laziness?): in France the figure stands at around 30%. I imagine Britain scores a little better than the USA, but probably not much, especially as mainstream UK publishing seems very much in thrall to American sales. Some of the most interesting translated literature is now being published by smaller, independent houses run by dedicated enthusiasts, but it's still only a fraction of what we should have available to us.

Anglophone readers have the advantage of a 'world language', but also the disadvantage. By not speaking other languages and not laying ourselves open to the literary products of other languages, we tend to be less mentally flexible and deprive ourselves of insights into other cultures that knowing their languages can provide. The situation is probably beyond rescue, especially now that foreign languages are given such a low priority in most British state schools. (It appears to be less the case in the private sector, creating a newly privileged cultural and intellectual élite predicated on the ability to pay for a superior education.) Perhaps if key celebrities and film stars were to be shown speaking or reading a foreign language, young people might demand the right to do the same ... which is pie-in-the sky: learning a language requires effort. It's harder work than shopping or watching TV or writing on Facebook about what you've shopped for and watched on TV. (Is that the spirit of a grumpy old woman I see before me? Probably.)

A modest proposal.

All the world's politicians – including presidents, prime ministers, and dictators – should be obliged, by their terms of employment and their country's membership of the UN, to spend a set number of hours each week reading books from other cultures. Most of these, of course, would be in translation.

Translations are rarely perfect, but they help provide insights into other 'ways of being', other histories, other ways of understanding or shaping experience. We should raise our translators to the status of national and international heroes. We should be devouring translations so that they have a hard time keeping up with the demand as we try to get inside the heads and experiences of all the diverse people with whom we share the planet. Might it not make a peaceful, just, and rewarding co-existence a little more possible? – though only if the politicians … (Can you imagine it? No, nor can I, really.)

Immersing ourselves in other cultures' views and experiences can make the world strange to us in the same important way as snow. *Ostranenie.*

'It's not going to snow. Forget it!' Malcolm says.

But I can't.

The waking up and knowing, from the quality of light seeping through the bedroom curtains, or through that little gap where they weren't quite closed properly, that it has snowed in the night. The still child-like (or childish?) excitement, the *absolute need* to go out in it, to wonder at it, play with it (though without spoiling too much of it). But hooked onto this immediacy is something else, something that has built up over one's years of reading – all the pleasures of all the snows one has experienced vicariously (though nonetheless intensely for that) through the words of writers, as well as through painted and photographic representations of snow. The two-way process of reading and art, a dialogue created between experiences, memories and the representations of snow, each enhancing the other. The more experiences one has of snow, the more one has to bring to the reading of snow, and the more one 'reads snow', the more the experience is made richer and deeper with acquired memories. Though we may read with an irrecoverable intensity when young, acquiring experience and knowledge through reading before we have lived a great deal in the world, there's a great case (as I said earlier) to be made for re-reading key books at different periods of our life. This can be dangerous, of course: books we remember dazzling us at eighteen, of radically influencing how we thought then, may suddenly seem callow or boring when re-read at forty. Or we can suddenly realise, in the light of lived experience, we'd completely misunderstood them in our youth. Others, of course, give us even more than they did in youth. The one exception for me (and others I've mentioned it to) is D. H. Lawrence. We agreed it was inspiring to read him as a teenager or a student, but we wished we'd let it become a happy memory and never returned to them. One friend was really scathing: 'They read like cranky bilge later in life'. I'm not sure I'd go that far, but maybe that particular reader was angry to 'see through' one of the idols of her youth.

I still like some of his poetry, though.

I have to admit to not doing enough re-reading. But I've just bought a new copy of *War and Peace* in which the print is larger than my old Penguin Classics edition. I'm saving it for when I go into hospital for the three to four weeks of the stem-cell transplant I'll need at the end of the chemotherapy. I'm relying on Tolstoy to get me through. My Chilean friend is currently re-reading it and her enthusiasm and delight in it have persuaded me that out of all the books I need to re-read, this must top the list. I hope it works ... though I may take some others – things I haven't read, things for a contrast – just in case.

While on the subject of *War and Peace*, last year I read *Natasha's Dance* – and have just lent it to my Chilean friend as a side-dish to Tolstoy – a wonderful cultural history of the novel's period by Orlando Figes (son of another writer I hugely admire, the late Eva Figes: try her *Light*, if you don't already know her work – especially if you've visited Monet's house at Giverny – and her autobiographical *Tales of Innocence and Experience*). A visiting friend alerted me to Figes' *The Whisperers* which is about Stalin's Russia, and at the time of writing I'm about a third of the way through it. Another marvellous insight, full of fascinating human detail in the attempt to understand the period, so far as we are able. A few months ago I read Masha Gessen's *Two Babushkas: How My*

Grandmothers Survived Hitler's War and Stalin's Peace, an insightful introduction to some of the ground covered by Figes in a different way (though still through personal stories). Gessen's book is the story of two women in the Soviet regime, one survives by (reluctantly) becoming a censor, therefore part of the repression, while the other becomes a dissident, risking her life for her principles.

Russia. Russian winters. The thought of all that snow. I keep checking the meteorological predictions: not a hope, not this far south, anyway. I'll have to have literary snow instead. I dig out some snow passages and scour our art books for my favourite snow paintings.

I re-read the snow description a few pages into Jean Cocteau's *Les Enfants Terribles* – the transformation of a certain part of Paris by snow. Then on to Orhan Pamuk's novel called simply *Snow*, and re-read his description of being on a Turkish bus driving into a blizzard, and other snowy bits of the novel.

And then to Boris Pasternak's story, 'The Childhood of Luvers':

Occasional snowflakes were floating out of the night, swarming towards the street-lamp, swimming around it, wriggling, then falling away; others swam up to replace them. The street glistened, as if paved with snow

– which promised ideal conditions for sleighing. [...]
Winter had come to Ekaterinburg. She turned her eyes
to the courtyard and started to think about Pushkin.

... which reminds me of a lovely extract in Nabokov's
autobiographical *Speak, Memory*, also picturing the
snow in the streetlights – this time in St Petersburg,
describing how the snow 'passed and repassed with a
graceful, almost deliberately slowed motion' and the
feeling of being in a room on that snowy afternoon
with the light fading.

And then I remember there's a short snow passage
in my own novel, *Zade*. With only a vague recollection of 'how it went', I pull that off the shelf, too.

On the morning of Christmas Eve it began to snow –
great soft flakes that soon lay light and deep on top of
one another in every place where no one walked or no
cars passed. There were bolsters on the window-sills,
duvets on the roofs, new white sheets spread in public
spaces – the city turned into a gigantic bedding factory,
with more and more white stuffing delivered from the
huge grey machine of the sky, itself hidden by its own
exorbitant production of whiteness. [...]

It was a relief to get out of the apartment with its
heavy tapestry of emotions, and into the simple cool
linen of the snow. Though twice my normal size with the
padding of jumpers under my usually loose duffle-coat,

along with the big woollen scarf, beret, mittens, thick socks and boots, I felt very tiny once I was out in the huge snowy landscape. A stiff little plastic figure in a glass-globe snow-scene being agitated by an unseen hand.

(The last sentence makes me smile a little ruefully: it's rather like I feel now – shut up in a little world controlled by the unseen hand of the disease and its treatment.)

But after snow comes the thaw. Especially those Russian thaws. I remember the one in my first ever Russian book, borrowed from that poky little room (described earlier) one life-changing, wet November afternoon.

After the thaw (which Karl Ivanych referred to as 'the son succeeding the father') the weather had been balmy, warm and bright for about three days. Not a sign of any snow on the streets. The filthy slush on the roads had been replaced by a shiny, wet surface and fast-running little streams of water. The remaining icicles hanging from eaves were melting rapidly in the sunshine; in the garden, the trees showed swelling buds; the path crossing the courtyard to the stables – passing a pile of frozen manure – was dry; and soft green sprigs of grass were sprouting between the stones around the porch. It was that special period of the spring that evokes the greatest response in the human spirit – everything gleaming in the brilliant sunlight, even though the sun wasn't yet giving off much heat. There were little streams and puddles where the snow had melted. The air was scented with freshness, and a sky of fragile blue was painted with the lightest of clouds. I'm not sure why, but the effect of these initial stirrings of the spring's arrival always seem more noticeable and amazing in a big city: although you see less of it, you feel its promise more keenly.

And then I have my own promise of a thaw, of new life. The results of the latest tests are good. Very good. Almost better than could have been hoped for. I can afford to be given a two-week break from chemotherapy over Christmas and New Year.

∽ SEVEN ∾

REASONS TO BE CHEERFUL: ONE

The bag I keep packed (nightdress, toothbrush, flannel, spare knickers, book, notebook, two biros) is only for the hospital – in case of another sudden dash – and not because I expect to be arrested by the NKVD. I'm not living (or going to die) in Stalin's Russia … though it's recent enough to have overlapped with my life. Just. I'm not going to be tortured and shot, though utterly innocent. There are much worse things than cancer.

After two morale-boosting weeks' holiday from chemo over Christmas and New Year, I'm back on it again.

This last week I have been to hell and back.

… To hell and back with the Russian people and the unimaginable scale of the physical and emotional sufferings inflicted upon them both by Stalin and the Nazi invasion. I've now finished Orlando Figes' *The Whisperers: Private Life in Stalin's Russia* – a ground-breaking study. Gruelling, fascinating, and opening windows of knowledge and understanding onto the processes at work in that particular bit of recent history through the detailed evidence of personal stories and records. Unbounded admiration for Figes' magisterial work.

But, as so often in reading, it's the momentary personal connection that strikes a match against you, as it were – that creates a spark of connection through some possibly trivial detail … in this case a brief sentence in the chapter on The Great Terror (1937-38), when even the most loyal Stalinists were not safe and could only passively await a cruel and unjustified fate. '*Many packed a bag and kept it by their bed in order to be ready when the NKVD knocked at the door.*'

I've had such an easy, happy life. My bag is for the clean new hospital that has all the drugs I need.

I think of that Chinese curse: 'May you live in interesting times'. I'm thankful they haven't been too interesting for me.

Hitler. Stalin. It seems unbelievable.

'*How lucky it is for rulers that men cannot think.*' Thus spake Adolph Hitler.

The duty to think. Always. To question. To acquire knowledge to help in the thinking. To put oneself in the company of intelligent friends, among whom one can number the writers of the books one reads. To do this for the purposes of developing one's ability to think. *Not to be taken in.*

Future message to the grandchildren. *Reading is not a luxury; it's a necessity. Read. Know. Think. Be alert. Live attentively.*

If only there were more time.

('How do you find the time to read?' A long time ago I gave up ironing sheets and knickers and handkerchiefs and have tried explaining why to my mother … who has always ironed them. Reading has set me free, to some extent anyway, from the chains of yesterday. There are always small, meaningless tasks or TV programmes one can forego in order to read.)

I already knew of the stark horrors of the Stalinist gulags from reading Alexander Solzhenitsyn's *A Day in the Life of Ivan Denisovich* when it first came out and made many of my students read it, too, over the years. Powerful fiction as their way into the history that's shaped our present world. And I'd read his *Cancer Ward*, but not *August 1914* or *The Gulag Archipelago*, usually considered his other two greatest works and which lots and lots of people were reading at the time. Why had I never got around to reading them? (The same guilt I always feel for never having finished *The Brothers Karamazov*.) But then looking at the dates when they came out I can guess why in terms of personal biography. Babies.

It's all a bit 'hit and miss', what we read and what we

don't read, and therefore the world view we develop. Serendipitous choices in bookshops, recommendations from friends, some of which are forgotten and others remembered. What we can afford. What's in the bargain bin. What's in the local library. What's going on in our lives when certain books first appear. And it's hit and miss as to what gets published – the personal whims of editors, the advertising budgets, the necessary pandering to 'the market' and the forces that create it. How do we know there aren't countless wonderful pieces of literature stuffed away in drawers and suitcases? … like Irène Nemirovsky's *Suite Française*, unread for sixty-four years. Nemirovsky was a successful writer living in Paris. She had only completed two volumes of a projected five-part novel on life in France during the Second World War when, being of Jewish descent, she became a victim of the Nazis. Her daughters managed to escape from France, with the manuscript. It was finally published in 2006.

A few years ago we found ourselves in a large London bookshop that was running an event called 'The Day of the Unread'. It was a display of manuscripts garnered from publishers and agents, I suppose – scripts that hadn't 'made it' into print and hadn't been returned to their originators. A lot of them were children's books with varying levels of competence in their illustrations (not to mention the words). It was easy to laugh at the ambitions of some of the more hopeless cases. Yet there was something tremendously affecting about all the effort that had been put into these still births. The urge to communicate what was felt to be worthwhile in the form of stories. The ardent wish to be identified as an author, to 'have a book out'. Just like children in school who, even now, love to make books, love to see their work in the form of a book. Something that can be held in the hand, put in the pocket. It's both sad and peculiarly encouraging to realise that the books that *do* get published are only the minutest tip of the vastest iceberg of those that are actually written. And those that are actually written, completed, are just a fraction of those begun and not finished. And those begun and not finished just a small proportion of the 'ideas for a book' that never get further than a note on the back of an envelope, a title lurking in the head, a vague idea … People die with them still in their heads.

As a civilisation, we remain in love with 'the book'.

REASONS TO BE CHEERFUL: TWO

Sea-horses are so beautiful.

SEVEN

REASONS TO BE CHEERFUL: THREE

I'm free to write what I like. If I want to say something as obvious as 'sea-horses are so beautiful', I can, without the fear of being suspected of using it as a code for something sinister or punishable. If I want to criticise the government, I can. If I want to campaign for a better deal for the world's women, I can. If I want to wear make-up and nail-varnish I can. If I want to wear shorts in public, want to have lunch with a man not my husband, brother, father, want to read books by Salman Rushdie, I can.

I've just finished Azar Nafisi's *Reading Lolita in Tehran*. I've had it for a while and the friend who gave it to me is coming to visit. Though slightly resentful, at first, from the feeling of compulsion after several weeks of reading exactly what I felt like, I was soon glad of the obligation – though the anger it aroused regarding the treatment of women under extreme, fundamentalist versions of Islam (for whose core, real values of mercy and love I have the deepest respect) probably wasn't good for my blood pressure. One already knew it in an abstract, theoretical kind of way, but once the facts are embodied in the stories of vividly-drawn individuals, once we share the real details of their personal lives and difficulties, their frustrations, fears, griefs, physical sufferings, that knowledge becomes written into our own flesh through words.

Nafisi – educated in Europe and the US, a professor of English literature – was teaching at the University of Tehran. When a new Islamic directive demanded that *all* women adopt the veil, she refused and was thrown out. Eventually persuaded that her teaching skills were needed more now than ever by young people growing up under an increasingly repressive regime, she compromised, going to teach at another university. Though she had to wear a head-scarf, she made a point of wearing it with subversive carelessness. The upshot of all this was her decision to start a book study group in her own flat, a group consisting of specially invited female students.

Reading Lolita in Tehran documents various changes in Iranian society (including the impact of the Iran-Iraq war) as well as the discussions she has with her students through her university lectures and her private group. The discussions are usually heated, partisan, dominated so often by the social and political context in a way that reminds us of the on-going relevance of literature from the past to what might seem the most unlikely contemporary situations. An affirmation of the worth of great literature as an object of close consideration and debate.

It's not only Nabokov's *Lolita* that the students

are presented with but Scott Fitzgerald's *The Great Gatsby* and novels by Henry James and Jane Austen. But it was some of the discussion of Nabokov that performed a valuable function for me: it got me back into fiction.

I've read *Lolita* several times and his autobiographical work, *Speak, Memory* (probably my favourite among his books) three times, and quite a few of his other novels once or twice. But I'd never read *Invitation to a Beheading*, which is discussed briefly by Nafisi and her students. It prompted me to get hold of it at once. And after just a few sentences I remembered what it was like to be in the hands of a really masterful story-teller and realised I didn't have a problem with fiction after all: only with fiction that's less than the best. Perhaps it's an effect of getting older and being aware that one's time is possibly limited. Why waste it on the second-rate? I know Nabokov isn't to everyone's taste, but his breath-taking twists and turns of language, his humour, originality, urbanity, sensitivity, daring … it all just takes me somewhere that I enjoy being. I feel it sharpening my mind and perceptions, changing the angle, raising the creative stakes.

So …

REASONS TO BE CHEERFUL: FOUR

I've rediscovered the joy of fiction. (Thank you, Nafisi … and Nabokov.)

∾ EIGHT ∾

When I was nine years old, I set out to learn an encyclopædia by heart – just one of those single-volume children's encyclopædias that are really glorified dictionaries. I only got as far as ALBATROSS and have never forgotten its twelve-foot wing-span. Some time later, studying *The Rime of the Ancient Mariner* at school, I was the only one in the class to have even heard of an albatross, but, with my precise knowledge of its likely size, I had great difficulty with the image of one being hung around a man's neck. With a twelve-foot wing-span, it was rather more than a large sea-gull. No wonder the mariner needed to talk about it!

Raising this question of the actual size of the albatross with the teacher, she tried to explain the concept of poetic truth as opposed to absolute, literal truth. She possibly used the term poetic licence. Couldn't he just have made it a seagull, I asked. She said that would have been too ordinary. It had to be a bird that was grand and special and rare so the mariner's crime in shooting it would seem all the greater. And anyway, the word 'seagull' doesn't have the same ring about it as 'albatross': and the rhythm's different. Coleridge would've had to change the wording of so many verses to make 'seagull' fit. Why? Just listen, she said, and chose some verses containing the word 'albatross', read each one, first in the correct version, then substituting 'seagull'. She'd made her point.

Many years later I recalled my 'albatross' dilemma when trying to explain the point and value of fiction to my ultra-factually-minded father – the way that fiction writers change truth to make it truer, to make the impact of its basic truth more incisive, to communicate it more effectively. Each recounting of a dreadful day at work to gain a spouse's sympathy, let's say, will involve exaggerations, elaborations, little deviations from the absolute truth to make sure the true emotional impact of the day upon us is fully felt and appreciated by the listener. Truth via untruth. Emotional truth. Poetic truth.

My father was a great believer in reading. 'If you can read, you can do anything.' (One of his mantras.) And he proved it. With little formal education, he became the world's top expert in his field, advising governments and the UN. But he didn't like fiction and couldn't really understand my commitment to it. It was a gap in our love for each other – a gap I wanted to close. It would have been helpful if, at the time, I'd had Mary Midgely's *Owl of Minerva* to hand: in it she paraphrases Iris Murdoch's argument that the imagination and its works are not just a luxury for the amusement of humanists. The imagination is itself 'a vital organ, a workshop where we forge our views of the world and thereby our actions.' One respected philosopher quoting another. Not mere novelists defending their trade. Not a slightly silly daughter 'without her feet on the ground'.

He enjoyed reading history books, so I tried another approach. These, too, were a kind of fiction, I suggested – a story told through the lens of one particular consciousness, that of the historian, who is likely to have a particular view of events. A history of the Second World War is likely to come out differently from the pens of historians from England, France, Russia, Germany, etc. As with biographies and autobiographies: no matter how earnest the attempt to tell 'the truth', it will be *a* truth. This is nowhere more evident than in writings about the revolution in artistic practice and social mores promoted by the Bloomsbury group. Those with 'class' issues on their mind dislike the upper class accents in which those radical changes were conducted. Another case is that of Sylvia Plath: feminists tend to give a different 'reading' of her life from non-feminists.

But my father was a hard man to convince.

I'm thinking of him particularly at the moment: it would have been his birthday this week. (He died of cancer just over two years before my own diagnosis.)

Another example I could have given him but didn't think of at the time was that of the ants. For something I was writing I once needed to look up facts about them. There was plenty in the INSECTS entry of my 1961 edition of the *Encyclopædia Britannica* (purchased second-hand for £50). In among the exhaustive facts of ant evolution and life was a curious paragraph that went like this:

> *But the forms of* Lasius niger *and relatives have never been successfully monographed. They are so similar, so abundant and commonplace, so uninteresting in their cloudy colours, dirty yellows, browns and grays, that ant students pass them by for the obvious rarities. In appearance of mediocre size, of colour, of structure they are merely uninteresting drudges in smelly nests. The brilliant colours, the size and above all the brilliant dash and resourceful individualistic behaviour of their distant digger-wasp ancestors has disappeared. All are alike. All have sunk in evolution to mediocrity of appearance and behaviour. They work in gangs and succeed as gangsters. Thus in the highest level of insectean evolution brilliant individualism has vanished. Widespread mediocrity has supplanted it — a mediocrity that is successful in co-operative groups. Is this mediocrity the certain fate of protoplasm in its evolution as a steadily-improved energy-*

*transforming mechanism? Will the mediocre gang in
the final social evolution of other animals eventually
supplant brilliant individualism?*

Now what *is* going on here?! This isn't straightforward information about ants. This is Professor X of the University of Y giving us his take on *human* life! And it isn't hard to see where he's coming from. Never a candidate, one would say, to have appeared before Senator McCarthy's House Committee on Un-American Activities. Is he just on about 'class'? Or is it, at the time of the Cold War, a dig at the USSR? (For one mustn't forget that, despite its title, the *Encyclopædia Britannica* is an American publication: they spell 'grey' with an 'a'.)

Long after forgetting the fascinating details of ant life, this paragraph remains with me in all its metaphorical dismissiveness of the lives of ordinary people whose daily labour maintains an economy which can pay professors to study the anatomy of ants. I want to slap Professor X.

But at least he reminds one to be alert to 'who is speaking' when we're reading a book (fact or fiction), an article, something on the internet. What axes do the writers have to grind? Where are they coming from? What fictions are they making around their facts?

My father had an interest in the Bible as an historical document – an interest developed quite late in life – and was happy to read certain aspects of it in terms of 'poetic truths', regarding many incidents as metaphors (such as the New Testament miracles: the curing of blindness he saw as the wisdom of love curing mental blindness, for example). But he couldn't seem to take it any further, couldn't transfer it to ordinary fiction.

Then I realised it was probably partly to do with the *kind* of fiction he'd encountered: middle-brow, pot-boiling, 'man's' stuff, mainly, thrust upon him by well-meaning friends who thought he'd enjoy it as much as they did. (Which shows how little they understood his mind.) And now it was too late: the damage was done. He'd made up his mind and was not a man to change it easily.

Okay, so I didn't expect him to read *Ulysses*: neither a minimal, pre-war state education (he left school at thirteen, turning fourteen – the youngest at which you could leave school then – during the Christmas holidays) nor his family background had equipped him for such things. Sometimes I longed to talk to him properly about *my* reading interests, not just *his* Biblical researches. It's true that when I finally had a novel published he was, apparently, very proud (so his friends told me later). After his death I found, on a shelf in his study, the copy I had inscribed to him. The bookmark was between pages twelve and thirteen.

What did I expect? He was a business man, and it was his gargantuan efforts that had supported my education and enabled me to become a 'book person'. He'd gone from office boy to company chairman (as you could, then, without a university education ... or any other qualifications, come to that) by hard work and natural intelligence. He was an autodidact. In a sense he was a first generation immigrant from a land – a social class – where children left school while still children, to a land, a class, whose children went to university. On the morning that my son got his 'A' level results confirming a place at Cambridge, my father cried.

He was a practical man who could build and mend and create things with his hands – including the enormous roll-top desk at which I'm writing this. He designed the house we moved to in 1962 (and where, at the time of writing, my mother still lives with his benign ghost) – a house he called 'Longwood' after the house on the tiny island of St Helena, in the mid-Atlantic, where Napoleon was imprisoned by the English after his defeat at Waterloo. (An important business solution he'd come up with regarding work for the people of St Helena had led to a promotion and rise in salary that enabled him to afford the new house.) On my first trip to Paris with my parents, we'd scoured the *bouquinistes* along the Seine for books or pictures of Napoleon's 'Longwood'. We finally found an aged paper-back, *Le Dernier Voyage de Napoleon: de Malmaison à Longwood*, by Las Cases, which contained one tiny landscape drawing with the house just visible in the far distance. It gave no idea of the sheer nastiness of the place, which I was about to discover.

A few months before he died, I found for my father a newly-published translation from French of a recent book, *The Dark Room at Longwood* by Jean-Paul Kauffman (translated by Patricia Clancy). It was another book he didn't read. I noticed it, pristine, during a visit to my mother's house during my Christmas break from chemo. I knew he wouldn't have minded me taking it back.

Kauffman is a journalist who spent three years of incarceration as a kidnap victim in Beirut, so is eminently suited to write about Napoleon's imprisonment on St Helena. Kauffman doesn't mention his own imprisonment in the main body of the text: we are simply told about it in the biographical notes and in the blurb on the back of the book. But we read everything with the knowledge of his empathy for the sufferings of the imprisoned – the boredom, the frustrations, the fears, the rages that come from being in such a position. (So, there I was, in my state of mild personal incarceration, reading a book by someone who'd experienced a much worse incarceration about a person who knew his incarceration would end only with his death on that prison island from which there was not any hope of escape. Ever. Reason to be cheerful. For *me* to be cheerful, that is.)

It was such a shame my father didn't get around to reading it: I think he'd have really enjoyed it – as I have, even though I don't think it's always brilliantly written (and it's unfair to blame the translation without seeing the original). And I can't help the suspicion that the two old English ladies who dog Kauffman's exploration of the island might be, in part at least, a fictional device (or at least a considerable enhancement of the truth) to enable him to have a further dig at the British – though of course I could be wrong. There is one searing moment when Amy, the more voluble and irritating of the two ladies (sisters, it finally turns out), remarks on the luck of the island's prisoners who enjoy the freedom to go fishing and play sports outside the prison walls, under the not-too-watchful eye of a dozing warder. Kauffman points out that the guards can sleep because they know the prisoners can't possibly escape from the island; they're entirely 'without hope' and that such prisoners are like dead men. Amy responds to this with, 'Ah, yes! Mr Answer-for-everything. How would you know? You know everything about Napoleon and now you're holding forth pedantically about people in prison.' He turns his back on her but her companion, says Kauffman 'has a strange look on her face as she looks intently at mine.' What's behind that strange look? Has she recognised him from media pictures as the former hostage? Or does she simply suspect him of being an ex-convict? This is as near as Kauffman gets to making reference to his ordeal. The book is the stronger for his reticence.

On the other hand, maybe my father wouldn't have enjoyed it so very much: the British don't come off too well and my father was fiercely patriotic – but not the kind of patriotic that had any truck whatsoever with racism: because he travelled widely for his job he was at home with people of every colour, race and religion – though he had an eternal bone to pick with the French, often telling the story of how, during the war, in a snowy France and Belgium, the Belgians would clear the snow from the roads onto the pavements to help the allies get through more easily, while the French dumped the snow on the roads, to keep the pavements clear for themselves. If my father had been in charge of Napoleon's fate, I wonder which impulse would have won: the instinct for revenge, or a British decency and honourableness?

Kauffman's book reminds me that Napoleon actually surrendered himself to the British when he could have escaped to South America. He believed their sense of honour would lead the British to hold him captive in some modest but pleasant English mansion. He did not expect the nasty revenge of the unhealthy and boring prison island of St Helena, nor the cramped and poorly-built accommodation of 'Longwood'. A non-French writer might have strongly defended the decision: though deprived of power, a Napoleon living a relatively free and healthy life in Europe was always in danger of making some sort of a comeback, wasn't he, or at least of *influencing* people with his thoughts and plans for a united Europe.

My father was against 'Europe' – that is, the EEC. A bone of contention between us. A subject best avoided. I tried to empathise. The war. He'd been in the RAF: all his friends had been killed; he just couldn't trust Germany. And I've even wondered whether calling his house 'Longwood' was a kind of celebration of the defeat of Napoleon and what he stood for. But he didn't really think like that. And I don't suppose he knew much about what Napoleon really *did* stand for – except that he was a Frenchman and the English had fought him. That was possibly enough.

He loved to talk politics – which was often hard because, growing up in the 60s, I was coming from somewhere quite different from him. When he saw a copy of *The Communist Manifesto* emerge from my satchel one evening he was convinced I'd be expelled from the excellent convent school they'd gone to such lengths to get me (a non-Catholic) into, his genuine agitation only confirming, for me, the power and importance of the book. Of books. As when books are banned or burned. It's a huge compliment, even though so distressing, worrying, terrifying, stupid.

The *Manifesto* was a book that changed the way I understood the world, of course it was. Though I never for one moment thought that what Marx intended had anything to do with Stalin. For a start, he had written specifically against the use of slave labour ... on which Stalin's Russia so massively relied. It's the recurrent problem with the 'big ideas' in books getting into the wrong hands, being taken, turned, corrupted, used to inspire and justify abominations: Christianity (the Inquisition; the Crusades); Islam (Al-Qaida); Nietzsche (Hitler); Marx (Stalin); Freud (we all have problems now and probably need a therapist). The dangerous, negative power of books. Once ideas are 'out in the world' in the easily disseminative form, they take on a life of their own. Books change lives, for worse as well as for better. Though mainly for the better. Let's be cheerful!

Going back to the point about my father not being able to relate to fiction. It was, ironically, as much him as my poetry-and-fiction-reading mother who gave me 'literature' because he gave me worlds beyond my own, gave me other stories.

A huge brown leather suitcase in the middle of the lounge of our suburban house. The corners of the case are reinforced with patches of darker leather – like the patches on the elbows of the 'sports jacket' my father was allowed to wear to the office on Saturday mornings (many people still worked more than a five-day week then). There were many coloured stickers on the case, insignia of a dozen different airlines.

An hour before, we had arrived home from meeting him at London airport after his three-month business trip to the Far East – his first time out of Europe. (I was so excited about his return I was sick in the hired car on the way there).

I wondered why the case was left in the middle of the room, not taken upstairs with the others so my mother could sort out the dirty washing and hang up his suits.

And then he opened it, and it turned from a brown suitcase into a magical treasure chest of gifts which didn't look or smell or feel like anything I'd ever seen before.

I can still conjure the sweet scent of the sandalwood fan, painted with birds and flowers (the smell of 'the East' will always be sandalwood for me); I still have the little string slippers, their fronts sewn with pale pink sequins and tiny pearls; for years I used the collapsible waste-paper basket from Hong Kong, each of its eight sides a different appliquéd, whispy-bearded Chinaman in traditional dress. And there were dolls in national costume from every country visited; I remember the elaborate dress of the Japanese lady; can still feel the stiffness of the 'butterfly sleeves' on the traditional Philippine dress; still remember the black woollen pig-tails of the doll from Hong Kong with her removable 'pyjamas'; the slightly broken, long, thin fingers of the two Siamese dancers made from papier mâché; can see the strange, rather scary face of the Indonesian shadow-puppet; can smell the slightly musty cloth doll from India in her turquoise sari and the tiny silver bead at the side of her nose.

For my mother there were delicate nightdresses and negligées in palest pink and powder blue, so utterly different from her usual modest cotton and winceyette that I was almost shocked when she wore them (they were rather transparent). A gold bracelet of linked butterflies from Japan. Silver bracelets and brooches from Bangkok. From the Philippines, delicate, embroidered napkins and place-mats made from pineapple fibre; and a lampshade made from the fine pearly slithers of *capiz* shells; an exquisite black-lacquered coffee set from Japan, each cup and saucer painted with minute landscapes. A tiny, hollow bean containing a dozen Indian elephants carved with breath-taking precision from the smallest scraps of ivory. (My father took my six-year-old hand and emptied the bean into my palm: 'Look! You can hold a dozen elephants in your hand!')

Later, when the films came back from processing, there were slide-shows of his travels: a traffic-jam of improbable, bright-painted 'jeepneys' in Manila; several shots of Mount Fuji taken from a moving train (each with a telegraph pole at a different point in the frame as he tried to get the perfect shot between the poles); the floating market of Bangkok; the temples and Buddhas; the 'Star' ferry and fishing junks in Hong Kong harbour ... and every picture had its story.

But before the slides came back from processing, there were other stories – stories you had to make up the pictures to in your mind, using only his words.

Some of the stories were funny (like trying to get a goat into a taxi for some reason); some alarming (the deadly snakes, the head-hunters of Borneo), and then the one that's haunted me all my life – a story that changed my awareness of the world, even at six years old.

The story takes place in Calcutta, 1955. My father's hotel is not in a good area of the city (his Scottish boss didn't believe in indulging his travelling staff). The view from his hotel window – I remember the photo he took from it – was one of chaos and poverty. Half-collapsed buildings, the roads a mess of rotting vegetation, rubbish, and cow dung, stalls selling fruit or drab bits of clothing, and stark-ribbed 'sacred' cows wandering among it all. You could almost smell it from that photograph.

Just after he'd taken the picture, while he was still coming to terms with the sudden plunge into this new location after the relative order of British Hong Kong, he noticed an old man, thin beyond belief and wearing nothing but a filthy rag as a loin-cloth, gazing at a fruit stall and at the cow helping itself while the owner looked on: as the animal is sacred to Hindus, he had to allow it to eat. The old man, clearly starving, could resist temptation no longer, grabbed a piece of fruit from the stall and tried to make off with it. But the stall owner and the people around had seen him and, too weak to evade them but struggling against their attempts to wrest the stolen fruit from him, the old man soon buckled and was on the ground. They probably didn't have to kick and beat him very hard to kill him.

When a policeman arrived on the scene, the crowd quickly drew back, leaving the dead man, now deprived of the very last vestige of humanity – the cloth that had been covering his private parts – alone in the middle of the filthy road. Seeming reluctant to touch him to check for signs of life, the policeman used his foot to try to stir the man, rolling him onto his side. But as soon as the foot was removed, the body flopped onto its back again. After a while, a cart arrived and two men, looking little more robust than the corpse they were dealing with, lifted him and threw him on.

… which is partly a little exercise in writing – and reading.

My father's actual account was closer to, 'In Calcutta I saw a man lynched for stealing a piece of fruit when the cows were allowed to help themselves.' Even those bare facts, along with my father's obvious distress when he spoke of it, showed me a world I had never seen before – showed me someone else's 'story'. But the truth of the awfulness of such an event needs to be properly 'embodied' if it's to make a suitable impact. 'Good fictions can tell the truth more trenchantly,' I'm saying to the ghost of my father. 'You could see the man being killed "in your head" because you were there, but to fully communicate what that meant to you at the time, you need to "do something with it".' Good fiction can be more effective in moving the reader to act – or at least to think – in response to a raised anger, outrage or love than a dozen political tracts or sociological studies full of abstract language and concepts, necessary as they might be.

But why didn't I choose to tell the story of the goat and the taxi? Why upset myself – and, potentially, the reader – by going on about that single death so long ago and so far away?

❧ NINE ❧

So long as men can breathe, or eyes can see,
So long lives this, and this gives life to thee.

The end of Shakespeare's (probably most famous) sonnet, 'Shall I compare thee to a summer's day'. An assertion of the immortality conferred by writing – both for the subject and the writer. A common enough idea: writing to leave some trace of the self in the world after leaving it. Or some trace of the persons (even an unknown, starving Indian), places, events or ideas written about. Probably not very dignified to admit it, these days, that one writes partly to avoid total disappearance from the world after death: a bit 'naff', a bit old-fashioned. Living, as we do now, with the constant background knowledge of the vast stretches of time and unimaginable hugeness of the universe, any brief after-life from fame as a writer seems more than laughable.

Then you could say that goes for human life altogether – and yet we cling to it! I'm trying to read some more scientific things to help me keep a purchase on 'proportion', trying to calm my panicking body into accepting its minuteness and lack of significance.

I pull off the shelf a little book about the stars – amazing pictures and full of overwhelming facts (which I can only assume are correct): for example, if you were able to drive a car through space at 100 km per hour, it would take you 170 years to reach the sun, and 46,000,000 years to reach the nearest star *in our galaxy*. After a few pages, I can't take any more and end up just looking at the pictures. Then I turn to something more substantial. In *LIFE: an unauthorised biography*, Richard Fortey points out that the 'narrative of life' has lasted more than 3,000,000,000 (that's three thousand million) years and that trying to express such ungraspable vastnesses of time in homely metaphors – such as a clock-face, mankind emerging at just one minute to midnight – only serves to trivialise a magnitude which should be held in awe. (Does that mean he would have disapproved of the 'homely' car driving through space example? I actually thought it was quite good at conveying 'awe'.)

The book was fascinating, but it still didn't stop my bodily panic. I know my brief presence on a rather small planet in a modest-sized galaxy in an ungraspably vast universe is much less than half a twitch of a flea's little toe, and yet … And yet we're desperate to hang on to our flickering little spark of life, even after we've done our duty to the species, reproduced to make sure our genes go on.

We have to decide whether we're going to consider human life as being worth nothing ... or everything. Or everything within that nothingness. Everything because of that nothingness. Worth more because of the vastness and nothingness that surrounds us. Hanging onto the wonder of it as well as the horror. Considering the harsh conditions in which so many human beings are forced to live, relatively few choose the escape-route of suicide. Not that many people actually *want* to die. I turn back to 'literature' and, as usual, Shakespeare hits the nail on its flat, round, workaday head in *Measure for Measure*:

> *The weariest and most loathèd worldly life*
> *That age, ache, penury and imprisonment*
> *Can lay on nature is a paradise*
> *To what we fear of death.*

Though, being Shakespeare, he also expresses the opposite view in the same play.

> *The best of rest is sleep,*
> *And that thou oft provok'st: yet grossly fear'st*
> *Thy death, which is no more.*

I think back to the first night of my first stay in hospital. Some time after the lights had been dimmed for the night (it's never ever dark in hospital), a wailing voice started up from the adjacent ward. I think it was female.

'I don't want to die ... Oh, please don't let me die ... Please don't let me die ... I don't want to die ... I don't want to die ... '

First reaction: annoyance. Impossible to sleep. The voice was disturbing everyone. Even poor little Elsie was shifting in her bed. And it's undignified, such yelling. You have to be *brave* in hospital: it's what everyone expects. Stiff upper lip and all that ...

Then I began to warm to the honesty of it. Wasn't that what we were all doing, inside, yelling 'I don't want to die'? Otherwise, what were we doing in hospital, trying to be cured? Like pop-singers singing our love for us, or footballers playing out our tribal urges, or writers putting down on paper our own observations of life ('what oft was thought but ne'er so well express'd', as Alexander Pope neatly put it), this honest voice was yelling into the night for all of us. The voice behind the urge to create something to remain in the world, something more permanent than flesh.

One reason why people write. In *Nothing to be Frightened Of*, Julian Barnes imagines a psycho-therapist telling him that his fear of death is bound up with his literary activities; that he makes up stories so that his name and some part of his unique personhood will remain in the world after his physical disappearance, and that this provides him with some comfort.

And people aren't content to just 'write'; they want to be published, want to be *read*. The god-like power of the reader: to deliver that longed-for immortality to the writer. By being influenced by what we read, by having our minds and actions in some way modified by the writer's vision allows the writer to go on acting in the world – acting *on* the world – though dead. Harold Bloom puts it rather nicely in *The Western Canon*: a poem, novel, or play, he says, takes on all the disorders of humanity, including our fear of our own mortality, 'which in the art of literature is transmuted into the quest to be canonical, to join communal or societal memory.'

> *So long as men can breathe, or eyes can see,*
> *So long lives this ...*

I need a bit of light relief. Stalin's Russia is still hanging over me, and thinking so much about my lost father and the vastness of the universe ... none of it is helping the depressive effects of some of the chemo. Time to reach for that Christmas present: Jeremy Mercer's *Books, Baguettes and Bedbugs: The Left Bank World of Shakespeare and Co.*

Mercer, a Canadian journalist, escapes to Paris to avoid a possible revenge attack threatened by a criminal. Penniless, he ends up staying (like so many other penniless writers through the decades) at the famous Left Bank bookshop run by the eccentric and humane George Whitman, called 'Shakespeare and Co.', after Sylvia Beach's original establishment that played host to (and sometimes published) such writers as James Joyce, Gertrude Stein and Ernest Hemingway.

'George's' shop is extraordinary, terrifying (how it's only caught fire once, I'll never know), magical, inspiring, irritating, smelly, and utterly irresistible. Malcolm and I have often visited the shop – more as a ritual homage to a phenomenon we approve of than to actually buy books there. We love the idea of the absolute, almost *crazy* commitment of George Whitman to his vision, his ideals. A breath from another world, one in the eye for the increasingly corporate rat-race that characterises the modern book 'industry'. And there's something about the crooked floors, over-loaded labyrinth of bookshelves, creaky, narrow stairs and the idealism that reminds us of being young, being students, being full of literary hope and political ardour, of having a life-time of reading and writing ahead.

Mercer gives an insider's account of the life of 'Shakespeare and Co', most of it not usually seen by the casual visitor or customer. The people who live there, free, in various little fetid beds in odd corners of the establishment. The wonderfully humane and generous spirit of its owner – even if his culinary skills include sweeping the husks of kitchen cockroaches into the dish 'for extra protein'. The condition of the one shared loo sends some inmates to the nearest café. But above all one loves George's unshakeable belief in the humanising power of books: he presses the best of them upon his guests, who are supposed to commit to reading one book a day in return for free board and lodging. A pleasant romp of a book blending familiarity with some new, behind-the-scenes insights.

(Like all 'living legends', the amazing George Whitman finally had to become just a legend: he died in 2011, aged ninety-eight. But his daughter, Sylvia Whitman, has taken over the shop – which is still thriving.)

I want to stay light and I want to be intelligently charmed, so next I plump for a Daniel Pennac, in translation this time: *The Dictator and the Hammock* – translated by Patricia Clancy. Even if I hadn't already known his work, the review extract on the back cover would have sold it to me at once: 'His masters are Denis Diderot and Laurence Sterne'. (Diderot alone would have done it.)

How to sum up this playful, quirky, entertaining, and ultimately moving book? – a book about dictators and doubles and look-alikes, about peasant suffering in South America (with a glance at 'magic realism'), about cinema, about Rudolph Valentino and Charlie Chaplin and Hitler, about human hopes and dreams and America as the land of dreams but also of greed, destructiveness, inhumanity. About the writing of stories and how authors create characters and situations out of the stuff of their own life: 'From the unpredictable and essential combination of thematic demands, narrative requirements, deposits left by life experiences, the vagaries of daydreams, the arcane mysteries of fickle memory, events, books, images, people … '

And you're never sure what's real and what's unreal: a character we're convinced is a real acquaintance of the writer is suddenly revealed to be yet another fictional construct as the story moves between high fantasy to the viscerally real description of a sleeping tramp in a Paris *Métro* station. Everyone is avoiding him, looking away, not because of the smell but because his flies are open and his penis hanging out. The female friend with the author at the time, we're told, 'stops when she reaches him, leans over, puts his penis back into his trousers, also tucks in the ends of his shirt, zips up his fly and buckles his belt …'

A gesture of moving humanity that inspires the creation of a character in the story who performs a comparable (though different) act of deep kindness and delicacy.

The book also made me want to watch the whole of Chaplin's film *The Great Dictator*. I've only ever seen brief clips. It's good when a book leads us to something else.

Still don't want to tackle anything too heavy for the moment. (There's *War and Peace* waiting for me! That long hospital stay may not be too far away now.)

Having started to write about my reading, I should revisit some of the books I've already read on the subject. My favourite is Alberto Manguel's *A History of Reading* – my copy littered with bright pink marks in the margins, its back inside cover filled with notes and page references made with the same fluorescent pen (not my usual choice: what was behind that?!). But Manguel would approve: books, he believes, are there to be read, written in, used. In his *Into the Looking-Glass World*, Manguel refers to his use of the endpapers of his Pléiade edition of Borges' stories for making notes on.

From my son I borrow my 2002 Christmas present to him, Francis Spufford's *The Child That Books Built*. A friend recommends a couple of others, including

Brought to Book: The Balance of Books and Life by Ian Breakwell and Paul Hammond: the web gets me a secondhand copy for £4.

I should also probably look again at Phyllis Rose's *The Year of Reading Proust* and maybe Alain de Botton's *How Proust Can Change Your Life*. Maybe.

Manguel's is a physically beautiful book – the cover, the many illustrations, the feel of the paper, the size of the print. Even the smell of it I like! He begins it with eighteen illustrations, from Classical times to the present, of people in the act of reading. He describes each briefly before saying, 'All these are readers, and their gestures, their craft, the pleasure, the responsibility and power they derive from reading are common with mine. I am not alone.' The sense of being part of a shared community of readers down through the ages, bringing to mind that moment in Alan Bennet's play, *The History Boys*, when the teacher talks about a hand from history reaching out to touch you with a description of an experience you thought unique to yourself.

As a detailed, wide-ranging and absorbing history of reading and readers, it's impossible to sum the book up briefly. And I can't recommend it enough. (It won France's prestigious Prix Médicis.) One of my favourite extracts concerns the readings conducted in Cuban cigar factories.

In 1865, the cigar-maker and poet Saturnino Martínez began publishing a newspaper (*La Aurora*) for the cigar industry workers. It contained not just features on politics but on science and literature, and published poems and short stories, too – including those by major Cuban writers of the time along with translations of well-known European authors. The paper also exposed the tyranny of factory owners and the sufferings of the workers. With literacy rates running at a mere 15%, to give everyone access to the paper's contents and to wider literature, Martínez came up with the idea of using a public reader. One of the workers was chosen as official lector. 'This way,' wrote Martínez, 'they will gradually become familiar with books, the source of everlasting friendship and great entertainment.'

Other factories also adopted the practice – which was so successful that it soon became regarded by those in power as subversive, and it wasn't long before the Governor of Cuba issued the following edict (14 May, 1866):

1.   It is forbidden to distract the workers of the tobacco shops, workshops and shops of all kinds with the reading of books and newspapers, or with discussions foreign to the work in which they are engaged.
2.   The police shall exercise constant vigilance to enforce this decree, and put at the disposal of my authority those

shop owners, representatives or managers who disobey this mandate so that they may be judged by the law according to the gravity of the case.

Despite this, some readings still took place in secret, though by 1870 they had more or less died out.

Reading as a subversive activity (because it leads to freedom). The novel under the desk at the back of the maths class. The torch under the bedclothes.

I liked the *idea* of Francis Spufford's *The Child That Books Built* more than the actual experience of reading it. Along with an often detailed revisiting of the books that dominated his childhood – particularly those by Tolkien, C. S. Lewis and Arthur Ransome – he also explores the reasons for his early plunge into reading: his younger sister had a continually life-threatening genetic disease which not only absorbed much of his parents' time, energy and attention but was also deeply distressing to witness. Books took him 'elsewhere', and he defines Lewis's *Chronicles of Narnia* as 'the Platonic Book of which other books were more or less imperfect shadows' (as they had been for my son). Books make life tolerable for him. He reads himself out of his situation and at the same time enriches his life.

I'm not sure why I didn't enjoy it more. Perhaps

our own childhood is so strong and deep in us that we can't quite take on that of others. Or maybe it was just too detailed an exploration of books we tend to be already very familiar with or which, while wonderful enough in their own right, were written for children. Or maybe we don't *want* our childhood books analysed and talked about. Perhaps we just want them whole and magical and how they were for *us*. But I'm avoiding having to face the main reason.

I think perhaps I couldn't overcome the anguish of a most heart-breaking coincidence. When I'd given my son the book, he and his wife had no children. By the time of my illness, they had two little girls, the younger having just been diagnosed as having the devastating handicap of Rett syndrome, sending her development backwards, depriving her of the ability to walk, to speak, to have virtually any control of her muscles, along with epilepsy and digestive problems … and she was born with a badly malfunctioning heart, a totally unrelated problem. Her brain, however, is fine. She understands a great deal, has a very developed sense of humour, loves books and music (especially jazz). But life is very, very hard for her and for her amazing parents. Her older sister, like Francis Spufford, is a voracious reader. But there the similarity ends. I have the strong impression she doesn't 'escape' into books, but that the empathy developed partly from her wide and sophisticated reading (as well as through the example of her parents) enables her to have a wonderfully loving and supportive relationship with her sister, as well as her parents. She has had to become very mature at a young age, bringing that maturity to her reading, and in turn bringing reading to her life.

I had bought the book for the title, because it seemed to fit my son, who'd grown up in a house full of books and writers. It was only now, on actually reading the book myself, that I realised the sad truth behind it – and the terrible coincidence. Some things in life are just too overwhelming and get in the way of any objective assessment of a book or one's ability to really appreciate it.

Nevertheless, there *were* some moments in Spufford's book I was able to enjoy. Reflecting on the impact of encountering a book at just the right time, Spufford uses the lovely image of a seed crystal 'dropped into our minds when they are exactly ready for it, like supersaturated solution, and suddenly we change.' And another delightful moment was his account of how the family's Danish *au pair*, after reading him the famous Winnie-the-Pooh story of going out into the snow and trying to catch the 'Woozle', actually takes little Francis out into the real snow, walks with him through a white-laden wood to 'find Piglet' … and there he is, 'perched on the hollow stump of an oak tree'. The *au pair* had sewn a toy Piglet for him and planted it in the wood. A wonderful moment for the child when story and world came together.

… which makes a convenient link with the 'Introduction' to Breakwell and Hammonds' anthology, *Brought to Book* where they make the link between the inner world of the imagination and the 'real' world beyond ourselves. They suggest that the two common ideas of how books 'take you out of yourself' – as an escape from the everyday into a more exciting make-believe, and as a way of lifting the reader out of self-centredness into a wider awareness of the world – are two sides of the same coin. It certainly reflects the two sides of the bibliotherapy I've prescribed for myself.

Breakwell and Hammonds' introduction is lively and humorous with entertaining booky anecdotes – like the Woody Allen joke of being struck in the chest by a falling Bible and saved by the bullet in his vest pocket, and the tenth-century Persian carrying his library on camels trained to walk in alphabetical order. As an anthology of (sometimes quirky and offbeat) pieces on books and reading, this is a lovely dip-in volume to keep around for odd moments.

... as is a delightful little present I'm given 'to cheer me up', called *Bizarre Books*, a themed anthology of, yes, very bizarre book titles and their publication details – all, we are assured by the collectors / editors, absolutely genuine. When I find myself losing my sense of humour, often in the middle of a wakeful night – the steroids don't give me much sleep – I reach for this book and have a quiet giggle in the still, dark house.

The vaguely obscene ones, in the section called 'They Didn't Really Mean It', get a bit tedious after a while (*Games You Can Play with Your Pussy*; *American Bottom Archeology*; *Erections on Allotments*; *Queer Doings in the Navy* etc., etc. ...), but there are some that simply fill you with wonder at the sheer scope and variety of what human beings know – and write books about: I adore *Wall-Paintings by Snake Charmers in Tanganyika*, along with *Selected Themes and Icons from Spanish Literature: Of Beards, Shoes, Cucumbers, and Leprosy* and *Anthropometric Measurements of Brazilian Feet*. And then there's *A Toddler's Guide to the Rubber Industry*, not to mention *On the Composition of a Mangold-wurzel Kept for Two Years* and *The Home-Life and Economic Status of the Double-Crested Cormorant* ... It all goes to show that humans really do find life on this planet, in all its forms and details, very, very interesting – despite the overwhelming size of the universe.

But I need something more substantial, something to get my teeth into, something to absorb and distract. No, I don't feel like re-reading *How Proust Can Change Your Life* … nor *The Year of Reading Proust*. Not for the moment. I may come back to them later. I want to go somewhere completely different. Somewhere like …

∽ TEN ∾

… Istanbul.

My first visit to the city, as a teenager, was in the company of a gentleman called Alexander Kinglake, an interesting and observant – and occasionally humorous – travelling companion, though a lot of what he had to offer was certainly lost on me at the time. Turkey was the first stop on an unforgettable journey around the Middle East.

Kinglake's *Eothen* was a class reader in our fourth year at secondary school. It was still Constantinople, of course, in Kinglake's time (the year was 1844). It was an odd book to present us with, even then (heaven knows what most of today's teenagers would do if seriously expected to read it!) yet its flavour stayed with me more deeply than did the more likely adolescent food of *Pride and Prejudice* and *Silas Marner*.

Why? Perhaps simply because it was so *different*. To send well-disciplined, identically-dressed school-girls on such a precarious adventure around the Middle East of the nineteenth century – a journey full of plague and cutlass-carrying Turks, and many another heart-stopping danger – was perhaps a stroke of genius on the part of the teacher. Or maybe it was all that was left in the cupboard – a set book for some distantly past examination and, mercifully, enough of them for the whole class. A serendipitous felicity. A safe way to broaden horizons, allowing encounters with the utterly different (and possibly dangerous) from the relative physical safety of the classroom.

With my incurable, possibly perverse need to possess the books I've read, I managed to find a copy of *Eothen* in a second-hand book shop. And even a brief dip into it yielded up treasures I'd utterly missed in the naïve, uninformed days of my first reading. (Yes, you should *definitely* re-read favourite books at different ages, no matter how well you think you remember them.)

A taster of Kinglake.

CHAPTER III

CONSTANTINOPLE

Even if we don't take part in the chant about "mosques and minarets," we can still yield praises to Stamboul. We can chant about the harbour; we can say and sing that nowhere else does the sea come so home to a city:

there are no pebbly shores – no sand-bars – no slimy river-beds – no black canals – no locks nor docks to divide the very heart of the place from the deep waters. If, being in the noisiest mart of Stamboul, you would stroll to the quiet side of the way amidst those cypresses opposite, you will cross the fathomless Bosphorous; if you would go from your hotel to the bazaars, you must pass by the bright blue pathway of the Golden Horn, that can carry a thousand sail of the line. You are accustomed to the gondolas that glide among the palaces of St Mark, but here, at Stamboul, it is a hundred-and-twenty-gun ship that meets you in the street. Venice strains out from the steadfast land, and in old times would send forth the Chief of State to woo and wed the reluctant sea; but the stormy bride of the Doge is the bowing slave of the Sultan – she comes to his feet with the treasures of the world – she bears him from palace to palace – by some unfailing witchcraft, she entices the breezes to follow her, and fan the pale cheek of her lord – she lifts his armed navies to the very gates of his garden – she watches the walls of his Serail – she stifles the intrigues of his Ministers – she quiets the scandals of his Court – she extinguishes his rivals, and hushes his naughty wives all one by one. So vast are the wonders of the deep!

I'll return to that long penultimate sentence in a minute.

It's hard to make the colourful, exotic, chaotic world of *Eothen* tie up with the sadder, somewhat elegiac account of the modern city in Pamuk's auto-biographical portrait of the city in his *Istanbul*. To try to get some sort of purchase on the history of the city and of the Ottoman Empire in general, I read Philip Mansel's *Constantinople: city of the world's desire, 1453–1924* – not a quick read but a totally engrossing one, a book to change, for ever, the way one sees a place, its history, its relationship with the rest of the world, and which helps illuminate the challenges for the modern Turkish state.

At the micro level, it also threw a lurid light on that penultimate sentence of the section from *Eothen* quoted above, and changes one's understanding of Kinglake's tone. Mansel makes many references to the standard way of disposing of 'unwanted' human beings – whether high-ranking court officials or wives or hapless young girls from the harem who had aroused displeasure in some way. They would be put into a bag and dropped into the Bosphorous. With this knowledge in mind, Kinglake's image of the Bosphorous as the bowing female slave of the Sultan becomes charged with menacing irony. (I'm sure our fourth-year English teacher did not point this out to us.) In his Istanbul, Pamuk, too, refers to the bodies of murdered harem girls being taken under cover of darkness and thrown into the waters of the Golden Horn. But at least in Pamuk's version they were already dead when thrown into the water – which had not always been the case according to Mansel. But alongside the cruelty, there was much else. In the early history of the city, the sumptuous materials, the exquisite architecture, the food, the gold and silver, the ceramics, the splendour of the ceremonies are all witness to the grandeur of the Ottoman Empire.

Barbarity and beauty: the extremes of both have been eroded by time. Pamuk's mid-twentieth-century Istanbul is a monochrome place, its colours sapped, its confidence gone – but, happily, the city has experienced a vibrant resurgence since then to become, once again, a favourite destination of travellers from every part of the world, known for the beauty of its setting, its architecture, its food, its people.

But before leaving Istanbul, I must mention the problem of the dogs – greyish, nondescript animals that are the bane of the city council, though Pamuk can't help pitying 'these mad, lost creatures still clinging to their old turf'. (There's a hint of a metaphor here – for himself? – for the Turks? But perhaps not.) The dogs are not a recent problem: apparently Sultan Abdulmecid (reigned 1839–61) had them all taken to an island in the Sea of Marmara, but had to bring them back again, so great was the outcry from a population who believed that dogs were an essential part of a city's life – and its luck. A Middle Eastern proverb states that 'a city where dogs do not bark at night is a dead city'. When the Young Turks movement came to power, they too tried to rid the city of its dogs.

Why am I talking about dogs?

Perhaps because I can't forget the following image in Mansel's book, an image buried like an old bone in that part of my brain that hoards such things for when I need a metaphor. In the spring of 1910 the dogs were rounded up and again taken to an island. To begin with, they would come to the shore every time a boat passed. Then, for several nights, blood-curdling howls could be heard coming across the water. In the end, it seems, the survivors tore each other apart and the city slept soundly for a few months. But it wasn't long before little squeals were heard as puppies emerged on the outskirts of the city, born from the few dogs who'd escaped the 'round-up'. By 1913 the dogs were prop-erly back on the streets.

To what use might I put such an image? On a bad day, I might see the dogs as cancer cells we thought were disposed of, but sneaking back like puppies born of those stray survivors. On a good day, the dogs might be my survivor mentality, my hope, my positive attitude, all but quashed by the exigencies of chemotherapy, but sneaking back to flourish again. (Well done, you dogs! Keep it up!)

Istanbul. Is it a city I'll ever go to?

Sometimes I feel I've already been to Turkey. The vivid descriptions of Pamuk. The memorable film *Ozu*.

But why does Turkey grab me rather than … Albania … Roumania … Bulgaria ?

Near the end of *Constantinople* Mansel mentions the burning of Smyrna by the Turks (acting against the Greeks). The phrase 'burning of Smyrna', its internal rhyme making it memorable, touched on something from my past … something that …

The postcards!

I suddenly remember the postcards.

They're in a funny little cardboard box I rescued from my grandmother's big clear-out before she died. Apart from a 1937 copy of the *Manual of Seamanship* they're all I have left, besides memories, of my loving, good-tempered naval grandfather.

The postcards, mainly from the 1920s, are black and white. There are many of British shipyards and ports and other places connected with my grandfather's life in his own country. But there are others – reminders that his naval career took him to places someone of his background would never otherwise have had the chance to visit: one of Spain; eleven of Algiers; twenty of Turkey – all of Constantinople and the Bosphorous, except one, showing the ruins of the small port of Chanak after its bombardment by the British fleet during the First World War (on 5th May, 1917, to be precise: it's recorded on the back of the card in my grandfather's handwriting, which I remember so well from my birthday cards as a child). And there is one of the port of Mitylene, which a little research tells me is on the now Greek island of Lesbos. The photo shows a modest, not unattractive waterfront with a few small fishing boats. Along the bottom, printed on the harbour waters, is the caption: MITYLENE, TO WHICH THE GREEK ARMY HAS ESCAPED. The use of 'has' before 'escaped' gives it the urgency of a contemporary event. Why did they need to escape? What were they escaping from? Turn the card over. Grandfather's writing again: *Where the Greeks escaped to during the Burning of Smyrna by the Turks in December 1922.*

The Burning of Smyrna. For decades (until I read Philip Mansel's *Constantinople*) just a memorable phrase to me – with no historical context: just a terrible picture of a town on fire and the desperate need to escape it – an example of the effectiveness of a standard rhetorical device, the kind easily grasped by eleven-year-olds learning about poetry – the repeated sounds, 'urn' and 'yrn'. If the phrase had been 'the Destruction of Smyrna' or 'the Razing of Smyrna', I simply wouldn't have remembered either it or the postcard. (A reminder of the importance of aesthetics in writing.)

Malcolm and I once saw Orhan Pamuk speak at the South Bank. Even if it *was* part of a promotional tour for his latest book to be published in English translation, *Other Colours: essays and a story*, it isn't every day you get the chance to be in the presence of a Nobel Prize winner. The sheer pleasure of listening to a person of intelligence, sensitivity, thoughtfulness, courage.

Whether, having bought tickets for that event, we were put on some 'interested in Turkey' database, or whether for some other reason, we were informed of an event hosted by the Turkish Embassy at which Orhan Pamuk would be introducing a new edition of the semi-autobiographical novel *The Idle Years*, by Orhan Kemal, for which he had provided the foreword. We couldn't attend the event as it clashed with an already accepted invitation, but because Malcolm is a journalist and literature promoter, he was able to request an advance copy of the book – which I now manage to find on the 'books still to be read' pile in the corner of his office. (I read and enjoy it: set in the 1920s, it's a valuable insight into the struggles of the young in a time of social and political upheaval in the region.) Orhan Kemal (1914–1970) is the much-loved author of twenty-eight novels and ten collections of short stories, some of which have been made into films and plays; a literary prize has been established in his name and was awarded to Pamuk in 1983. Through reading Orhan Kemal, I discovered there are four well-known Kemals in Turkish literature, about two of whom I knew nothing: Namik Kemal (1840–1888: poet, translator, journalist, social reformer); and Yahya Kemal (1884–1958: poet and politician). But the Kemal I *had* previously known – Kemal number four – is Yashar Kemal (born 1923: novelist), the most famous of his many books probably being *Mehmet, My Hawk*, though my personal favourite is the brief but beautiful *The Birds Have Also Gone*.

And before I leave Istanbul, I must say a little something about that book. It centres on a group of poverty-stricken young boys who attempt to earn money by catching birds and selling them for release: apparently there's an old tradition that poor people of the city sell captured birds, 'in front of churches if they are Christians, synagogues if they are Jewish, or mosques if they are Moslem.' Customers pay to release the poor little creatures as an act of mercy, calling out as they free the birds, 'Fly little bird, free as the air, and meet me at the gates of Paradise.' But times are hard for the bird-sellers: people are just not interested any more (I won't tell you what happens). In an aside, the narrator expresses the opinion that if the chroniclers of Istanbul ignore the history of these birds and of those who catch them, he would consider their work as historians insignificant. 'The joy of millions of little birds set free in front of churches, synagogues and mosques for hundreds of years, and the joy of so many people, too … Is that an adventure of small importance?'

A reminder of the 'partiality' of histories, of how we reveal our values and priorities through what we include in them and what we leave out.

But I have most of the riches of Turkish literature still to discover. Even a brief trawl of the web shows there is so much … so much … And that's just *one* country. What about all the others I've missed out on or scarcely touched at all? So much to know, still, so much to enjoy, understand, experience. I want time. More time.

⚭ ELEVEN ⚬

'As you haven't got time to read all the books in the world, at least read *these*.' I suppose that's what we really mean by 'the canon': books that an awful lot of people who have read an awful lot of books (thoughtfully) consider worth dedicating a chunk of our brief time on this planet to reading.

Is 'the canon' the same as 'the classics'? One could argue the subtle differences, but life's too short. For the here and now, let's accept them as interchangeable, or just talk about 'great books' or 'books really, really worth reading'.

During the period when some academics were busy doing what they referred to as 'dismantling the canon', I happened to be attached to a university English department, for the purposes of research, so had to grapple with what was going on. There were some fierce and worthwhile debates which all seemed terribly important at the time. And some of them were, of course. Terribly important. An 'adjustment' of the literary canon to include more of the women writers who were at least as good as the men; to include other excluded voices – other ethnicities, for example.

Where I thought it *did* begin to get a bit silly was in the muddling (in lesser minds) of what might be of interest to 'cultural studies' with worthwhile literature. I'm sorry, but the flight of the sparrow through the lighted hall – that image, from Anglo-Saxon literature, for the brevity of human life – is too rapid to give much time to Barbara Cartland book-a-week production-line romances (to take the extreme) beyond acknowledging the social phenomenon that some women find solace in them. And even if those readers don't take them too seriously, just using them as a little holiday from everyday life, I have a sneaking suspicion that such stories are instrumental in perpetuating the difficulties of so many women's lives. I confess to being an old-fashioned feminist of the Simone de Beauvoir variety and I believe that, if you can, it's better to read *Middlemarch* and *Mrs Dalloway* … and *The Second Sex*. Their truth and honesty may be harder to face and to process but more liberating in the end. It's certainly easier to imagine oneself, in the tradition of those tired old romances, to be the down-trodden secretary who ends up marrying the boss, or the frumpy little nurse whose kindness and professionalism win the heart of the highly-paid and conveniently widowed-or-divorced surgeon. But when the book is closed and the 'holiday from life' is over, real life awaits, unchanged, and the reader has acquired no added mental or emotional equipment to help them change it. Because, at the end of the day, good books have the power to help change lives for the better. So I'm in favour of the kind of hierarchies of 'worth-reading-ness' that a canon implies.

But what *is* it about a book that gets it a place in the canon? What really *is* it that makes a writer 'great'? Nabokov believed that a writer is a story-teller, a teacher, or an enchanter, that a major writer combines all three, with the 'enchanter' aspect predominating. And he refers to the 'telltale tingle in the spine' that lets us know we are reading a great work of literature. We know what he means. But I'm not sure how helpful the 'tingle down the spine' is as a definition: it's only one step up from 'you know it when you see it' – rather like trying to define beauty.

Perhaps it's easier to say what a 'great book' *isn't*. A novel is unlikely to be 'great', believes Nabokov, if the writer's purpose was to 'improve the morals of his country' – to preach lofty ideals from a soapbox. Such an intention is likely to end up as 'a precarious heap of platitudes.' Great literature works upon the world less directly, such as when writers are able to 'make iniquity absurd' by using what might seem small details, or exaggerations that might at first glance seem irrelevant. (He gives the unforgettable example of portraying a tyrant, in his luxurious bedroom 'exploring a profitable nostril'.) Great writing and great writers, Nabokov reminds us (possibly thinking of himself) avoid 'the warty fat goblins of convention'.

The American critic Wayne Booth and the Canadian Northrop Frye would both seem to be in agreement with Nabokov on one point. Booth, in *The Company We Keep: an ethics of fiction*, focussing on the ethical transformations that can be brought about in us by literature, believes that the consequences and values we carry away from the experience of reading can often be most profound and effective when the reader 'has been least conscious of anything other than "aesthetic" involvement.' And in a similar vein, Northrop Frye, considering art in general, believes it is 'neither good nor bad, but a clairvoyant vision of the nature of both', and attempts to link it with morality are 'incredibly vulgar.'

But that's enough. One could go on for ever trying to define what, at the end of the day, escapes definition. Perhaps the best we can do is see the great classics, the books of the canon, the books most worth reading (whatever you want to call them) as those friends most worth keeping company with because they enrich us and our lives in ways that are sometimes describable, sometimes not.

I suppose the essential idea of the canon was, originally, that it should be unchanging, that the books included would be good for all time. But as the decades and the centuries roll on, new works inevitably need to be added – which can only mean that others become neglected and, in the end, no longer form part of the 'active' canon (like people dropping off your Christmas card list).

Imagine a balloon debate: four books in the basket of a rapidly descending balloon: one must go if disaster is to be averted and the rest survive. Which one would you tip over the edge? Let's say –

Sir Walter Scott's *Ivanhoe*
George Eliot's *Middlemarch*
James Joyce's *Ulysses*
Salman Rushdie's *Midnight's Children*

Personally, I wouldn't hesitate one second. *Ivanhoe* would go. But if the choice was between, maybe –

Chaucer's *Canterbury Tales*
Cervantes' *Don Quixote*
Tolstoy's *War and Peace*
Proust's *In Search of Lost Time*

I would agonise for ever, weep buckets at the thought of any one of them being lost.

It's a good game to play, even with lesser texts:

it makes you really think about what it is you love about a book. Or with the works of an individual author. Or even children's books ... *Wind in the Willows*, *Alice in Wonderland*, the Winnie the Pooh and Just William stories.

At the end of his great work of defence, *The Western Canon: the books and school of the ages*, Harold Bloom lists what he considers to be canonical books in four periods, following Giambattista Vico's division in his *Scienza Nuova* (The New Science, 1725) of cultural development into the Theocratic Age (power in the hands of religious leaders), the Aristocratic Age (power in the hands of an unelected elite), and the Democratic Age (those in power elected by the people). Bloom adds the Chaotic Age: our own. (Vico thought there would be a period of chaos before the emergence of the New Theocratic Age.) The number of books Bloom lists as canonical increases exponentially with each age: at a quick count I make it ninety-five for the Theocratic Age, two hundred and twenty-eight for the Aristocratic, three hundred and fifty-one for the Democratic, and seven hundred and seventy for our own Chaotic Age: this has not yet been through the sifting process of Time which ensures the survival of the fittest ... and only the fittest. (In his delightful collection of essays, *Why Read the Classics?*, Italo Calvino says our own times are too eclectic for us to be able to draw up a list of defining texts.) Bloom admits that, while he tries to keep personal preferences out of aesthetic judgements about a text's worthiness for the canon, there are elements of his own taste at work, especially in the most recent section. (I happened to notice the absence of George Orwell's *Animal Farm*, for example, though *Nineteen Eighty-Four* is included; Iris Murdoch is represented by two of her novels ... and not those which immediately come to my mind. There's an awful lot of Faulkner, but only two Nabokovs. And so on.) But Bloom's main focus is on just twenty-six authors (he omits texts from the Theocratic Age) which he considers to be the key ones for the Western Canon. Although I agree with most of the list, I would want to argue over one or two omissions. Here are the twenty-six. (See what you think.)

Shakespeare, Dante, Chaucer, Cervantes, Montaigne, Molière, Milton, Dr Johnson, Goethe, Wordsworth, Jane Austen, Walt Whitman, Emily Dickinson, Dickens, George Eliot, Tolstoy, Ibsen, Freud, Proust, James Joyce, Virginia Woolf, Kafka, Borges, Neruda, Pessoa, and Beckett.

What? No Flaubert? No Henry James? No Faulkner? No T. S. Eliot? Pleased as I am to see the poet Emily Dickinson on the list (bringing the number of women up to a grand total of four!), I personally would not put her there at the expense of Henry James, and although I like Neruda (sharing a surname with him before he changed it – he was born Neftalí Ricardo Reyes) and treasure my copy of his *Twenty Love Poems and a Song of Despair*, I would not include him in the canon at the expense of Italo Calvino or Dostoyevsky.

It's impossible to legislate entirely from outside the personal – especially when the choice of riches is so great.

Perhaps it's easier to say what shouldn't be included than what should. And there are bound to be a lot of 'fuzzy' areas. The image of a stone thrown into a pond may be useful: there's the big plop in the centre representing a culture's inescapably key texts (such as the Koran or the Bible or the *Odyssey* or the works of Shakespeare), and around this point are first deep ripples, then progressively less deep ones. Or one can think of a tapestry with its key, supporting threads over which a pattern is woven. Or …

But even the most dedicated of professionals are unlikely to have read all that Bloom lists. Italo Calvino starts off *Why Read the Classics?* by reassuring us, lest we feel inadequate in our ignorance, that however wide-ranging one's formative reading is, there will always be a huge number of fundamental works one hasn't read. And in typically playful Calvino style he goes on, 'Put your hand up anyone who has read the whole of Herodotus and Thucydides. And what about Saint-Simon? And Cardinal Retz?' He then attempts a number of statements that try to define what a classic is, elaborating briefly on each of those statements. My two favourites are number six – 'A classic is a book which has never exhausted all it has to say to its readers' – and number nine – 'Classics are books which, the more we think we know them through hearsay, the more original, unexpected, and innovative we find them when we actually read them.'

Calvino believes we should read the classics not because they serve a *purpose*, but simply because 'reading the classics is always better than not reading them', and reminds us of the story (apocryphal or not, it's a lovely one) that, while the hemlock was being prepared for Socrates, he busied himself with learning a melody on the flute. Someone asked him what use such a thing could be in his situation: his reply was, 'At least I will learn this melody before I die.'

But because there are just *so many* books worth reading, Calvino thinks the best thing is for each of us to invent our own ideal library of classics: his advice is to let half of it be made up of books we've already read and that have been important to us, while most of the rest should be books we intend to read because we think they *might* mean something to us – leaving a section free for surprises and chance discoveries

What would such a library of personal classics reveal to visitors about who we are? As a connoisseur of other people's bookshelves (at the expense of appearing horribly nosy) I've always thought you could tell much about their owners from what is found there. But Daniel Pennac has thrown my judgement into question. Speaking recently about his own library, he said it consists mainly of books he doesn't think much of. All the ones he really likes are out on loan to friends or have simply been given away in a gesture of altruistic enthusiasm to spread the books' pleasures as widely as possible – confirming him, in my eyes, as a man of great generosity and integrity. I wish I could match him: a few times, I have … but the loans tend to be 'mistaken for gifts' (I'm trying to put it in a nice way!) and, as I *need* my books around me, I'm ashamed to say that lending them to all but my closest friends is something I do less and less often.

I'm not going to list my personal classics. It's likely to be rather obvious (with a few little exceptions), and the waves are moving toward the pebbled shore (to borrow an image from a Shakespeare sonnet about 'mortality'). Instead of making that list, I could be reading another classic because, yes, I want to read more classics, and to re-read those read when much younger, knowing I'd get so much more out of them now. But more and more wonderful and necessary books are being published all the time. How to keep up? Always the thought, 'What am I missing?' Never enough *time* ...

And there's not just the Western canon to tackle: there's the Eastern canon, too – though harder of access, up to now, because the West has dominated the world book industry for all sorts of obvious reasons. In a 2005 *Paris Review* interview, Orhan Pamuk goes as far as to say that the Eastern canon 'is in ruins'. There are plenty of 'glorious texts' that have emerged from non-Western civilisations – Persian classics, not to mention Indian, Chinese, Japanese – he says, but there is a lack of will to publish them, to make them available to a world readership. The canon has long been in the hands of Western scholars, placed at the main centre of distribution and communication.

The hope is that with the growth spurt in the Chinese and Indian economies, and with the West's need to engage more effectively with the Arab world, there will be an impetus to rescue and re-erect the Eastern canon. I don't want to be ridiculously optimistic, but I think there are signs that it is already happening.

To tie in with the 2008 London Book fair, at which the 'Market Focus' was Arab Literature, there was a special edition of *Banipal* – an English language magazine of modern Arabic literature then celebrating its tenth anniversary. In her editorial, Margaret Obank summed up encouraging moves towards a greater genuine engagement between East and West, a new mood of wanting to develop proper dialogue and understanding with the Arab world through its literature. She discerned a mood of genuine interest and desire to learn, very different from the 'atmosphere of gross ignorance and disinterest' that was the norm when the magazine was started. And in this connection, literary translators, she said, are extremely underrated, for 'it is through their work that different cultures really get to know each other. In that sense literary translators are the interpreters of human values – and the true peacemakers.'

(Big cheer for that last sentence! Make it a compulsory epigraph for every translated work!)

Banipal deals with modern Arabic literature, but the magazine takes its name from Ashurbanipal, the last great king of Assyria and patron of the arts whose most magnificent achievement was surely to assemble in Nineveh, from all over his empire, the first systematically organised library in the ancient Middle East. An example of the modern leading one back to the glories of the past. And I think this could be symptomatic of what happens when we engage positively with the current literary products of a culture: it arouses our curiosity about its past, about its founding texts, its classics. So perhaps a demand for access to these texts will lead to a 'putting together of them' (as Pamuk calls it), a determined re-erection of the *other* half of the world's literary canon. It's a start that Penguin Books publish an *Anthology of Classical Arabic Literature* and also a number of classic Chinese texts – tasters that make us hungry for more.

Other good news for the wider acceptance and valuing of translated literature includes the establishing of various prizes – such as the Independent Foreign Fiction Prize, and *Banipal*'s own prize for translation from Arabic to English. Recent years have also seen the emergence of small presses dedicated to fiction in translation (such as And Other Stories and Peirene Press), and since 1989 Britain has had its own Centre for Literary Translation, founded by the late W. G. Sebald (at the University of East Anglia at Norwich), whose own literary fame in the English-speaking world rested on the skills of translators such as Anthea Bell and Michael Hamburger.

While *Banipal* was celebrating its tenth anniversary, Saqi Books (and the associated Al Saqi Bookshop, in West London) was celebrating its twenty-fifth. Founded in 1984 by energetic and inspirational childhood friends André Gaspard and the late Mai Ghoussoub (fleeing to Britain from the civil war in Lebanon), Saqi began by publishing academic and general interest books on the Middle East, soon expanding into general literature. Their publication of fine voices from North Africa and the Middle East has contributed significantly to the reassessment and wider appreciation of the Arabic heritage. Their list now includes writers from across the world and, before one bemoans the lack of female voices coming out of the East (which I found myself doing after having read my fourth book giving an insight into the lives of alienated young *males* in Arab societies), one could do worse than look at the volumes of short stories (under Saqi's 'Telegram' imprint) by, for example, Bangladeshi, Pakistani, and Iranian women. The name Al Saqi means 'the one who gives you water', referring to the men in souks and bazaars with an urn and cups who give water, usually free, to whoever is thirsty, and the emblem of Saqi Books – such an appropriate image – pictures a man pouring water and holding out a cup to two children. In 2008 the company won the first Arab-British Culture and Society Award.

But as with Europe, one should consider the purely national canons – of French literature, Italian, German … Lumping together cultures as different as Japan and Lebanon, for example, as 'the Eastern canon' seems at best unhelpful, at worst an insult. Canons within canons.

And stepping outside fiction, there are canons in other forms of writing to consider – canonical books of travel writing, of science writing, *et cetera*, *et cetera* …

So much. So many riches. Never enough time to get grips with the world, to understand it and all that is in it. Never enough *time* …

'Never, never, never, never, never.' (See *King Lear*.)

∾ TWELVE ∾

'Talk, talk … that's all you can do,' says Laverdure the parrot, with exquisite irony, to the humans around him in Raymond Queneau's soul-tickling *Zazie in the Metro* (English translation by Barbara Wright) – one of my all-time favourite novels.

And there are so many different *kinds* of talking – especially when it comes to books. Just reading a book isn't enough – not often, anyway. So, I'm thinking about some of the different kinds of talk relating to books. First there's …

The silent dialogue with the author / book that goes on in your head as you read. Authors give us information or experiences or a take on life that we reply to in our heads – accepting, disagreeing, immersing ourselves in what they're telling us, being amazed, wanting clarification. Not forgetting that the writer has actively sought this strange dialogue with the silent interlocutor – you – even though your replies will generally remain unheard by them … unless you are a book reviewer or one of those people (both loved and dreaded by authors) who write to them, personally, about their book. A book is only a *potential* dialogue until engaged with by the reader: the writer is at your mercy.

You could say that **a book starts off as a dialogue between the author and their subject matter.** Like any good conversation, the author is likely to be changed by the process of writing the book – just as we are likely to be changed, modified by our engagement with the book in some way. A mute but important and inescapable dialogue. Sometimes it moves up a notch to become …

A visible dialogue with the author/book – those notes we make in the margin, the underlinings, the lop-sided asterisks, the scribbles on the blank end-pages, the ideas, phrases, paragraphs marked then sometimes copied out into a notebook. Things we don't want to *lose*, a dialogue we want to be reminded of the moment we open the book again. This might develop into some kind of more formal and deliberate dialogue like …

Writing about the book – the kind and seriousness of the writing depending on your status – as student, academic, reviewer/critic, publisher's reader, blogger, or friend writing to friend. One of the reasons we remember so well (positively or negatively) the books we studied for past exams is that we were obliged to engage with them not only by listening to the teacher / lecturer, and discussing them in class or informally between fellow students, but in *writing*. However, those not in any of the 'writing' categories may have to make do with …

Listening to other people's dialogues with the author / book. This will generally take the form of reading reviews (including blogs or other online reviews) or listening to book discussion programmes on the radio or television. This is never an entirely passive form of engagement, however, especially if we've read the book under discussion. We match the responses of the 'discussees' to our own, or argue with them silently … or not silently. How often have you caught yourself joining in – refuting, agreeing, being appalled, suddenly realizing you've said something out loud like a mad person, you *talked to the television*, so engaged have you become with the discussion (… like my grandmother who would call out advice to characters on the screen: 'No! No! Don't go there! They're waiting for you! Watch out! Oh, you stupid man! Look behind you! …')

And while on the subject of listening to radio discussions of books, we mustn't forget the experience of **listening to books being read** – at one time just on the radio, but now on CDs and downloads, too.

'Book at Bedtime.' Radio 4. 10.45 p.m. Chemo fatigue means I've sometimes been too tired to read by that time. My first real experience of the 'B. at B.' phenomenon ... and of an even bigger one: a lady by the lovely name of Sally Marmion.

How many times have I drifted off to sleep to the lulling of the story-teller's voice, but resurfaced with the change to the business-like announcer telling us, at the end, that the novel had been 'abridged by Sally Marmion'. She's so prolific – prolific in her abridgements. A remarkable skill, to turn a book into exactly fifteen-minute chunks in multiples of five (for Mondays to Fridays). Bedtime stories for grown-ups, with the boring bits left out.

I try to imagine what's she's like, at first only able to envisage her back as she sits at her desk, all hours of the day and night, abridging ... abridging ... But then I manage to see her more fully, her name conjuring up a youngish woman with lots of shiny blond hair, comfortably built (not fat, just healthily fleshed) with rather a large, mobile mouth and expressive grey-blue eyes. Then, as I began to realise just *how much* abridging she's done, she metamorphoses into a lady of more mature years with short, neat brown hair and a pair of heavy-rimmed spectacles ... gaining even more years, after a while, to become a slightly younger version of Doris Lessing.

Disturbed by this shifting image of the admirable Sally Marmion, I try 'googling' her (wonderful eponym! – even better than 'wellies), but only get the titles of books read on Radio 4 that have been *abridged by Sally Marmion*.

Dear Sally Marmion, whatever you're like, whether you resemble any of my conjured images of you or not, you are a hero – up there with translators and with those who adapt great classical music for little, learning hands. True, I don't always like the books you abridge, but I now understand what a life-line they are for those whose eyes restrict them to 'large print' or who cannot read at all, or who, like me, are temporarily reliant on such pleasant but intelligent bed-time elsewhereness. You deserve your lovely, liquid name. And remaining just a name (I cannot find a picture of you), I play novelist and build a character around the name. The difference between seeing the film of the book and reading the book itself. I can invent you. And that's much more fun.

And so to something *un*abridged.

For years, my personal dialogue with James Joyce's *Ulysses* was a prickly, difficult, frustrating conversation that never got very far. I would start reading it every 16th June – known as Bloomsday because that date, in 1904, is when the events of the book take place as we follow Leopold Bloom (mainly) around Dublin. It's now a secular holiday in Ireland, with many celebrations in honour of Bloom's peregrinations around the city. After a few years I knew the opening by heart:

Stately, plump Buck Mulligan came from the stairhead, bearing a bowl of lather on which a mirror and a razor lay crossed. A yellow dressing-gown, ungirdled, was sustained gently behind him by the mild morning air. He held the bowl aloft and intoned …

Each year I got a little further, but that 'further' was never really very far (a third of the novel in the best year). I loved Joyce's other work. I loved the *idea* of *Ulysses*. I'd read a lot *about* it. But whether it was the size of the print or the bulk of the book (not good for handbag or pocket), or the lack of an ear for its Irish rhythms, I'd never, ever got to the end. Then, in the late 1990s, I discovered that Naxos had released (in 1994) a four-CD abridgement (or highlights), which was just a taster of things to come in 2004 – the *un*abridged, 22-CD version read by the same actor, Jim Norton (with Marcella Riordan as Molly Bloom). Experiencing the 'highlights' made me totally disregard the cost of the unabridged version (at no matter what cost, it would be beyond price: Jim Norton deserves whatever prizes are going for his truly *wondrous* rendering of the text) and I bought it for myself.

An awkward conversation turned into a love affair. For months I spent every night with Leopold Bloom, going to sleep with him, waking in the night and pressing 'play' to make him keep me company and drive away the persistent whispering in the dark that my dear, brave father, despite temporary remissions after chemotherapy, was going to die.

I've tried to make a list of adjectives to describe *Ulysses*. Here, in no particular order of importance, are some of them: REAL, SURREAL, HUMANE, RICH, VARIED, FUNNY, OUTRAGEOUS, OBSCENE, SACRILI-GIOUS, DELICATE, EMPATHETIC, POIGNANT, DISTURBING, TREMENDOUSLY-WELL-OBSERVED, HOPEFUL, A BLOW FOR FREEDOM AND HUMAN DECENCY (which is not exactly an adjective, of course, but an important effect of the book).

People (including people who should know better) love to repeat the jibe that *Ulysses* is the most famous book not to be read by anyone (or virtually no-one). Okay. But *hear* it – hear it as you were meant to hear it in your head – and you see why those who know what they're talking about call it one of the greatest literary works and a defining text of the twentieth century.

With Jim Norton as my interlocutor (helped by Marcella Riordan – her rendering of Molly Bloom's final monologue is just unforgettable), I look forward to the new discoveries, the fresh nuances to be found in the book's extraordinary richness each time I listen.

Yet some readings can damage one's dialogue with a text. I remember the horror and disappointment of hearing T. S. Eliot's recorded reading of *Four Quartets*. His pompous intoning had almost made me hate a poem I'd previously loved. Plath was better, but the strained American edge grates in some of the poems. My dialogue with these includes shouts of 'objection!' They don't sound as they do in my head. And even Shakespeare's plays are often better in my imagined productions than on a real stage.

Recordings apart, one is sometimes lucky enough to find oneself …

Listening to the author's own dialogue with his book/work. This can happen in radio or TV interviews, of course, but increasingly we get the opportunity to witness it in person. The veritable explosion of book / literature festivals, events in bookshops and libraries (as they try to drum up trade) and the gruelling promotional tours publishers now inflict upon their writers means there's often a well-known writer 'coming soon to a location near you'.

In *A Reading Diary*, Alberto Manguel records the experiences of re-reading favourite books, one each month over the period of a year, from *Wind in the Willows* to *Don Quixote*, from Kipling's *Kim* to Chateaubriand's *Memoirs from Beyond the Grave*. In his foreword to the diary, Manguel contrasts what the profession of writer used to be like ('solitary, slow and sensuous' – giving it much in common with good reading) with the current situation where writers have to be more like travelling salesmen cum repertory actors, performing one-night stands in far-flung locations, promoting the virtues of their books instead of toilet brushes or sets of encyclopædias.

I thought of this passage as I sat in the front row at the Purcell Rooms waiting for the start of a PEN event on 'The Rights of the Reader' – which was also part book promotion event. To my very good fortune it was to include three writers I hugely admire and about whom I've been writing here: Alberto Manguel, Daniel Pennac, and Asar Nafisi – the *Reading Lolita in Teheran* author – who, unfortunately, was unwell and could not participate after all. And yes, we really were right in the front row (a rare thing: we're usually in the 'gods' or the 'restricted view' seats), within smiling distance of the participants.

It's always given me a weird feeling to be in the actual presence of someone famous, someone I've known and admired at a distance, as if I'm watching a hologram of them while the *real* person remains tucked away somewhere in my head. (I remember the story of the woman who, having met the Queen, commented that she 'looked just the same as she does on the tele'.)

Manguel and Pennac were both as thoroughly decent and charming as their books suggest (… though it can work the other way round, too: I know a crime writer whose depiction of violence is so brutal and truly shocking I can't read it, but he's a charming, gentle, good-humoured man with a couple of delightful children to whom he's obviously a very good dad: the infinite *surprise* of people). Manguel, rather than extol the virtues of his own books in travelling salesman fashion, graciously chose to read from and comment on the absent Nafisi's work.

I can't reproduce much of the evening's conversation, but just remember the sheer pleasure of hearing good-natured, intelligent but non-academic talk about books and reading and writing. No point-scoring or nit-picking such as used to get me down at academic conferences. One just felt part of a valid and very pleasant tribe, open-minded, appreciative, and, yes, *happy*!

Afterwards, as I already had all of Manguel's books and most of the Pennac's that were on sale there, I bought Sarah Adams' translation of Pennac's *Comme un roman* (transmogrified, for the English, into *The Rights of the Reader*). I duly lined up to have my book signed and exchange a few words with my hero in nervous, slightly stumbling French. I told him how much I'd admired *Chagrin d'école*. He got me to spell my name (there's nothing like it in French) and, on the blank page at the front of the book drew four little stick people running with a banner that proclaimed 'VIVE HEATHER'. Long live Heather. You can imagine that it meant more to me than he'd intended – just as any writer's words can mean more (or less) than intended to a reader bringing to those words their own uniquely accumulated life or where they happen to 'be' at the time of encountering the writing.

Then there are those opportunities to meet authors *en masse*.

Book festivals (sometimes called 'literature festivals') are now almost as common as jumble sales were before the advent of charity shops. There are the big, established ones, of course, like Edinburgh, Hay and Cheltenham, and the more recent but still prestigious (partly because of location) Oxford and Brighton festivals. There are those just starting up in cities like York and Dundee and Coventry. There's the month-long, county-wide Essex Book Festival, while many modest towns have spawned admirable little festivals where small size and big quality often (though not always) go together. There's also the phenomenon of Wigtown – a tiny settlement of less than one thousand permanent residents but a lot of bookshops offering a quarter of a million (or so) books, old and new. And you can attend a ten-day festival of readings, performances, exhibitions and debates there, in the setting of Scotland's beautiful Galloway coast.

And the British book festival phenomenon is spreading across the world. There's Bloomsbury publisher Liz Calder's brainchild, the Parati International Literature Festival (often referred to as 'Flip', its Portuguese acronym), founded in 2003 and held in a small but beautiful Brazilian town halfway between Rio de Janeiro and São Paulo. It has rapidly established itself as an event where you can see a lot of big names.

But surely one of the most unexpected of book festivals is the 'Feria del Libro de Bogota' – the annual Bogota Book Festival, which is as old as Hay. Despite Colombia having one of the lowest literacy rates in the developing world, Bogota is often called 'the Athens of South America', and one famous library, in the city's Candelaria district, is the world's most attended library. At roughly seven thousand visits each day, it apparently outstrips the British Library, the Bibliothèque François Mitterand, and the New York Public Library. And in 2007 Bogota was a UNESCO designated World Book Capital. The title is given in recognition of the quality of a city's programmes for promoting literature and reading and the dedication of all players in the book industry. The cities it has been awarded to so far, starting in 2001, are Madrid, Alexandria, New Delhi, Antwerp, Montreal, Turin, Bogota, Amsterdam, Beirut, Ljubljana, Buenos Aires, Yerevan, Bangkok and Port Harcourt .

And then there are the many 'special subject' book festivals – like London's Festival of Asian Literature, Jewish Book Week, Spit-Lit (the Spitalfields Literary Festival, devoted to writing by women) and a growing number of festivals devoted to children's literature, many hooked onto adult book festivals (like Edinburgh and Brighton), but one or two existing in their own right, such as the Bath Children's Book Festival – not to mention those dedicated purely to poetry (the best known probably being those that take place at Aldeburgh and Ledbury, though there are many, many others). In fact, literature enthusiasts not burdened with earning a living could probably spend their entire lives going from festival to festival.

But why?

Why this *explosion* of book festivals in recent years at the same time that people regularly bemoan the decline in reading?

- Is it simply a trend encouraged by desperate publishers to secure some kind of continuing market for their wares?

- Is it a spin-off from that other explosion, in reader groups, many established by libraries equally desperate to reverse the decline in their issue numbers?

- Is it the thinking person's version of the wider celebrity obsession of our times? – the thrill of face-to-face contact with the 'famous' … or semi-famous in the case of some festivals?

- Is it that bookish people feel increasingly besieged in a society where priorities seem to be elsewhere? Do book festivals perform a reassuring 'gathering of the tribe' function for them?

- Do people go *to be seen to go* – to be able to tell people they've been (a tribal marking) … to help create an identity for themselves as 'the kind of people who go to book festivals' (therefore, surely, cultured, part of an élite).

- Something to do with the power pecking-order game? – rather than for *the thing in itself*? … though in the process they're laid open to *the thing in itself,* the book, the power of the book. And what's wrong with creating an identity through books, anyway? Better than wanting to create an identity out of how many cars we own or how much tax we can get away without paying. And each time we simply read a book in public, aren't we establishing an identity in the eyes of other people (so by reflection in our own)? – 'I'm the kind of person who reads Stephen King ... Joanna Trollope ... Jane Austen ... Philip Roth ... Salman Rushdie ... George Steiner ...'

• And do some even go to book events because they have no other more pressing commitments and it's better than what's on the telly?

Possibly a little of each.

What are the *outcomes* of the kind of encounter with writers one has at these festivals? Does the experience make one a better reader? Answer: possibly. In my own experience, encountering the actual face, body, and above all the voice of a writer tends to elicit a kind of openness – even tenderness – towards them and their work. It's very hard to be dismissive of a writer's work when in the presence of the fine eyes or charming smile or pleasantly self-deprecating manner or infectious enthusiasm or idiosyncratic laugh of the actual human being who created it.

And hearing work read in the voice of the author – the initiating voice of the text – can give access to a rhythm and tone we might have missed. I came to this conclusion a long time ago when lucky enough to attend a seminar given by great cultural historian and novelist, the late Raymond Williams (1921–1988). I'd long been an admirer of his work, the range and depth of his thought, but found his prose style difficult to the point of frequent abandonments. But hearing his voice as it expressed the rhythms of his thought – speaking quite slowly, reflectively, deliberatively, the subtle, judicious emphases making all things plain – I could suddenly read his work without effort … as long as I managed to hear it in his voice.

But as in the case of my distress at the recording of T. S. Eliot reading his own poetry, it can work the other way. Example: one of my heroines, Susan Sontag (1933–2004). I like the very *idea* of her, and even if I don't agree with *absolutely* everything she says in her non-fiction, I admire the breadth and depth of her mind and talent. When she was in London to promote one of her novels, we managed to get tickets for a bookshop event at which she was reading from and talking about this latest work. She herself was delightful, but I don't know if it was how she read or if it was the fault of the novel itself, but it sounded so flat and boring we didn't even buy a copy at the special event price.

There can be delightful surprises, though: virtually unknown writers whose events we've attended out of a sense of duty because the event was in our local library or bookshop, then been bowled over by the charm of the person which encouraged one to be open to their work and found unexpected delights.

I've been involved in book festivals as audience member, interviewer / chairwoman, ticket checker, book-seller, general dogsbody, and even as a writer, and each has had its moments of glory ... and of terror. (Sometimes both simultaneously.)

There was the event to which nobody but the organisers (who included Malcolm and myself) turned up ... followed by the excruciating train journey back to London with the very disgruntled author. (The sighting of his name in a bookshop can still make me feel a little queasy.)

There was the time I was designated to 'look after' Germaine Greer and a well-known Tory, in the same room, before a discussion event. My pre-event nightmares about scratched faces and the hair flying proved a waste of anxiety as both turned out to be the embodiment of gentleness and good humour ... to me, each other, and the world at large.

Even worse was the time I nearly passed out with nerves before interviewing Julian Barnes (I'd obsessively re-read his entire *œuvre* for the occasion and spent weeks structuring my interview questions) at a local festival event at which my entire A-level English class would be in the audience. Every single student loathed his *Flaubert's Parrot* (one of their set texts) and I dreaded what the more outspoken among them might say. Happily, they seemed so over-awed by being in the presence of 'fame' – albeit of the literary variety – that they were perfectly behaved and charming. They remained unreconciled to *Flaubert's Parrot*, but were less rude about its author now they'd met him and been photographed with him for the local press.

Then there was that tent at the Charleston Festival (held in the grounds of Charleston House, once owned by Virginia Woolf's sister, the artist Vanessa Bell). Some book festivals are, inevitably, very big on tents. The author we'd travelled so far and expensively to see, playwright Simon Gray (who'd been one of my teachers at Queen Mary College) was replaced by another at the last moment, due to illness. But this became of very little concern compared with the almost hurricane-force winds that were making the tent's main 'mast' begin to sway … just a little. Though convinced we were right in its path if the huge thing should topple, we nevertheless went on sitting there, like everyone else, with apparently total *sang froid*. Maybe no-one wanted to instigate a panic. Or maybe we all preferred to put dedication to words before risk to life and limb. How absolutely admirable! How utterly stupid! And I don't remember a thing stand-in celebrity, Jonathan Miller, said. I just remember the slight but sickening sway of that enormous pole and the sound of a huge wind beating the canvas …

(The brain wants life more than literature.)

At the end of the day these festivals are really just *celebrations* – aren't they? – of that totally amazing human invention: the book. And we're endlessly fascinated by our invention. It's easy to laugh (or groan) when an event, opened to questions from the audience to the writer, elicits the same ones you, as a frequent book event attendee, have heard a hundred times:

'Where do you get your ideas from?'

'Are your characters based on people you know?'

'Do you write by hand or on a computer?'

'How can I get my book published?'

'What advice would you give someone who wants to write a book?'

Questions that are both 'silly' and 'deep' at the same time. People really are simply fascinated by the whole process by which thoughts and visions that exist in one person's mind are transferred to other minds, all over the world, through the medium of 'the book'.

But a word of warning: if you are a newly published writer doing your first festival or some other book event, beware the slightly unnerving person in the front row (or sometimes the back row: they tend to go for the extremities) with the heavy-looking plastic carrier-bag: it contains the one and only copy of their *magnum opus* and it's for *you*. For you to read, recognise as a masterpiece, and use your 'connections' to get published. Be nice to them, but accept it at your peril! (Though who knows: perhaps it really *will* turn out to be the *Anna Karenina* of the twenty-first century.)

∽ THIRTEEN ∾

Late January.

I can't make myself swallow the very last tablet of the fourth three-week cycle. My body's simply had enough. That last tablet – it's the only thing I don't do that I'm supposed to.

Every day I've measured out my three litres of water and drunk it all … and more. I've written up my daily time-table of medication, stuck to it relentlessly, ticking off each dose as I go from the daily, self-administered stomach injection at 7 a.m. to the last tablet at 10.30 p.m. I've kept my weight up, as instructed (even gained some). But now I've had enough.

I'm struggling with Hermione Lee's biography of Edith Wharton, too. After nearly forty books read cover to cover since starting the treatment, I abandon it half way through. It's a fascinating biography but just too big and loaded with detail for my present state. I can't be bothered. It's exhausting me.

For the first time my consultant sees me miserable and even a bit weepy. He sympathises, assures me he understands what it's like, even though he hasn't been through it himself. I reply with something mawkish like, 'And I hope you never do.'

He gives me two weeks off while waiting for the results of the last tests. I could need up to six cycles, especially as they had to reduce the doses because of my over-sensitivity to the drugs.

After a few days off chemo, I begin to feel almost human again. We'll risk going away for a couple of days. Without the wheelchair. Not too far, but somewhere *different*: I want new experiences, new places after the months of near incarceration.

Stratford-upon-Avon. Despite our adoration of Shakespeare, we've never been there. (Perhaps, in fact, *because* of it – not wanting to see him turned into tea-rooms and tourist tat.) *Henry VI Part II* is on. Not a play we know well, so even better. We book tickets and a hotel near the theatre.

The production reminds us of the brilliance of the RSC – and the weather's even better: ridiculously warm for the time of year. People are walking about, dazed, in tee-shirts. The river is glimmering in the sunshine and we eat lunches on its banks.

I've got my legs back and manage the walk to Anne Hathaway's cottage, which turns out to be a lot less 'naff' than we'd feared. The guide uses the tour of the house to explain the derivation of various words and expressions. Fascinating.

In the garden, shrubs and herbs are beginning to come back to life and some spring flowers are out already. There's a butterfly (yes, a *butterfly!*) sunning itself on a wall. We're there early so have the place blissfully to ourselves. We stroll around the formal garden ... and see something that suddenly illuminates, makes concrete and physical, a couple of the most beautiful lines of *Twelfth Night* (Viola describing what she would do to convince another of her love) :

> *Make me a willow cabin at your gate,*
> *And call upon my soul within the house.*

There it was: a willow cabin! There really *was* such a thing – a little conical shelter woven of living willow. Not just a fanciful image after all: the real, living willow woven into the metaphor of the soul as the beloved. That spine-tingling meld of reality and imagination. The reality *in* the imagination. In the poetry of it.

Through the orchard and on into a meadow that has been made into a sculpture garden and a kind of tree exhibition. Characters and themes from Shakespeare, interpreted by many different sculptors, are set among trees mentioned in the plays. Each tree bears the quotation in which it appears. And every quote reminds us again just how rich, how astounding is Shakespeare's use of language. '*Zounds! I was never so bethumped with words ...*' And the sun is shining and I feel well and this glorious morning is the nearest thing to a worldly paradise.

We sit on a bench in the garden, happy in the moment. There's even a huge bumblebee. We watch him and smile. He looks disoriented (it's only just February) but purposeful. A little too purposeful when he detects our presence.

It's me he's after! I try to wave him away ... to dodge his clumsy, drunken dive-bombing. But he's persistent. Nothing I do will deflect him. He's attacking me. The last thing I need in my system at the moment is the poison of a bee sting. He really *won't* leave me alone.

There's only one thing for it: we have to leave. Ducking and flapping my arms, I stand up ... and run, chased away from that beautiful place, that fleeting, happy moment of life, by a very small but out-of-control bit of unseasonable nature, of the genus *Bombus* (hence 'bumble'), of the family *Apidae* ... But once again, the edge is taken off my panic by literature as, running, I call over my shoulder to Malcolm, slightly adapting Shakespeare's most famous stage direction to ...

Exit, pursued by a bee.

∽ FOURTEEN ∾

War and Peace. That new hardback copy I splashed out on ready for the long hospital stay. It looks as though I won't be needing it after all – not just yet, anyway. I'm in what they call 'near complete remission', which is a very good place to be, apparently, and as I'd had some bad reactions to the chemo and the kind used at the time of transplant is much more extreme, they're just going to stand back and watch me carefully to see what happens. It isn't a cure, of course – myeloma isn't yet one of the totally curable cancers – and I'll live the rest of my life, like Peter Pan, with a shadow stitched to my heel.

My stem-cells are harvested and will be kept frozen for future transplants (enough for two) – later rather than sooner, I hope, though it's unlikely to be more than two years at most, they say. During the harvest I make friends with the woman in the next bed who is having the same procedure, but she must have the transplant immediately. She's also a reader. I visit her in hospital. Unlike me, the initial chemo had scarcely affected her, but *this* … She can't even read a newspaper and just laughs when I mention my planned *War and Peace* coping strategy.

204

Panic!

Will I be the same?

If I can't even read, how will I rescue those hospital weeks – of necessity to be spent in an individual isolation room – from the oblivion of living only in the body? How grab back time from the disease and use it for enrichment, the way that's been possible these last difficult months? Will I even be able to concentrate on audiobooks? (Perhaps I should start buying some now.) … Or music? …

I must start making contingency plans, just in case.

Maybe it won't come to a transplant – though my dear consultant, knowing my dread, firmly tells me that when I *do* need the transplant – and I *will*, he emphasises – I'll just have to 'bite the bullet' and 'be philosophical' about it.

I want to say to him that being truly philosophical – engaging with the world in the way that actual philosophers do – isn't about *accepting* things: it's full of questioning, discomfort, anguish even, danger, searching, wondering, probing. Think of Socrates, Rousseau, Kierkegaard, Nietzsche, Sartre …

Of course I know, really, the sense in which he means it: try to adopt the long view, see it all in broader terms, with a sense of perspective and proportion on your own life … on human life in general.

In some ways it was easier to do that in the beginning: but now that I've had a taste of health again, and been presented with the possibility of more future health than was at first suggested, I find it harder. *I want more living.* I want more people, love, books, pictures, music, places, ideas, flowers, sunshine, food. As hungry for it all as I was at eighteen. All the reading I've done in such a short period *has* made life richer, has re-heightened the sense of the complexities and fascinations and infinite details and varieties of human life within the world ... whatever it all means. I love it all for itself, even if it *means* nothing at all, and I want more – much, much more ...

I should try to be more measured and restrained, shouldn't I? Maybe Montaigne will help. That first paperback I ever bought. A 'return to origins'.

The cover shows I paid seven shillings and sixpence of my pocket-money for it – about thirty-five pence ... for a brand new Penguin Classic: it was that long ago. Beneath the black band across the top of the cover, saying simply 'Penguin Classics 7/6 Montaigne Essays', is a famous portrait of Michel de Montaigne (1533–92), credited with having invented the essay form. The blurb on the back of the book explains that, attempting 'an entirely new, non-chronological method of autobiography,'

Montaigne aimed to 'test his responses to situations and to ascertain the permanence of his impressions and opinions. As he explores a huge range of subjects 'the man displayed is objectively detached, tireless in his search for truth, and at all times restrained.' And we're reminded that the inscription on the medal he so famously had struck for himself was *Que sçais-je?*- 'What do I know?' (implying 'I don't know much').

It seems I haven't read all the essays in the book. Only about two-thirds have been ticked off or bear the marks of reading. Some have clearly been read two or three times (notes and underlinings in different pens, different styles). I know the first essay well: 'That our actions should be judged by our intentions'. It made a big impact on me when I was fifteen or sixteen: a wonderful sense of freedom from responsibility *as long as one did one's best to do what seemed to be the right thing*. A great comfort to one who was often afraid of saying or doing the wrong thing without intending to.

The fourth essay in the book has also been ticked – 'That no man should be called happy until after his death' – but I have no memory of the content. It probably didn't seem so very urgent to a school-girl (even to the rather earnest one I suspect I was). According to Julian Barnes, in *Nothing to be Frightened Of,* it is with Montaigne that our modern thinking about death begins: he provides a connection between 'the wise exemplars of the Ancient World and our attempt to find a modern, grown-up, non-religious acceptance of our inevitable end.' As Death will always win eventually, the best defence, Montaigne believes, is to bear it constantly in mind. His position suggests that living with full and constant awareness of our mortality can enhance life, can make it more precious, luminous, *appreciated*. I can't quote him directly on that as the essay I'm thinking of doesn't appear in my modest Penguin collection (I once ploughed part of the way through an enormous edition of the *Essays* in a college library). But the truth is that it has hit home over the last few months as never before. Knowing the Grim Reaper isn't just coming up the road – as he is for everyone – but is 'lurking with intent' around one's very own front gate, makes every daisy on the back lawn a miraculous little sun.

Another of my heroes, Boris Vian, lived constantly with the taste of death in his mouth. With a serious heart condition since childhood, he knew he'd die young. It turned out to be thirty-seven, as mentioned earlier, but into that short life he packed more than most octogenarians have, his sense of Life intensified by the ever-present eye-beam of Death. The playfulness and exuberance of his novels, songs and poems often contain an undertow of mortality – more obvious in some than in others. But it's this that gives them their piquancy, their satisfying complexity, their *reality*. I think Vian and Montaigne would have a lot to say to each other.

But death is far from the only subject Montaigne writes about. One of the joys of reading him is the sheer breadth of the subjects he tackles. He can move from a lofty 'Defence of Seneca and Plutarch' to 'The custom of wearing clothes', from 'Vehicles' to 'Cannibals'. And here I must recommend two books on Montaigne: first, Terence Cave's little introduction to him, *How to Read Montaigne*, and a most wonderful study by Sarah Bakewell, *How to Live: A Life of Montaigne in one question and twenty attempts at an answer* – definitely a book to re-read … and to give to people you love, even if they don't know Montaigne.

The seventh essay in the Penguin collection, 'On the education of children', still strikes me as incredibly modern (apart from the fact that pupils are assumed to be male) and full of good sense and good humour. It's interesting to compare his ideas with those of nineteenth-century New England among such educators as Bronson Alcott, father of Louisa May Alcott of *Little Women* fame. (I've been reading a fascinating double biography of father and daughter by John Matteson, *Eden's Outcasts*.) But back to Montaigne.

Although 'On books' has been ticked off in the contents list, I don't remember anything about it, so decide to revisit the essay. Most of the essay records Montaigne's personal responses to some of the great Classical texts (more Romans than Greeks), but in the early part he gives a general portrait of the kind of reader he is. For him, books are above all about pleasure and he doesn't care to labour over difficult reading: 'What I do not see immediately,' he tells us, 'I see even less by persisting. Without lightness I achieve nothing.'

Lightness is generally a quality more appreciated in maturity than in youth, I suspect. Youth is the time for intensity, for big emotions, for taking oneself seriously … the time for D. H. Lawrence, Jean-Paul Sartre, Dostoyevsky, Solzhenitsyn. Then, in time, one comes to 'the unbearable lightness of being' (whether or not one reads Milan Kundera's novel of that name). And the next step is coming to love that lightness.

Lightness. Suddenly a thread is thrown between Montaigne in the sixteenth century and Italo Calvino's beautiful, posthumously published *Six Memos for the Next Millenium* (even the black and white cover is exquisite). It's based on a series of lectures he'd been preparing at the time of his death in 1985, and in them he identifies, recommends, explores and defends the qualities and values he considers the most important for the future of literature. Only five of the six were completed. In addition to Lightness, we have Quickness, Exactitude, Visibility, and Multiplicity (the sixth was to be Consistency). But 'Lightness' is the first – hence that thread I felt between two authors for whom I have a great and deep affection. Abolish the linearity of time and put these two in a room together: they'd have a great deal to say to one another.

Yes, Montaigne and Calvino … and invite Boris Vian, too. And would they get on with Nabokov? … or find him too patrician and full of himself? But Georges Perec, *he* should be there … And Denis Diderot …

And like a 'line of plain chant blossoming into polyphony' (a phrase I happened to hear on the radio this morning, describing a piece of music), my imagination begins to create an otherworldly party. With a kind of macabre joy and self-indulgent hubris, I turn it into a party to welcome me into the next world, whenever that might be. The guest-list is made up of the writers, artists, composers and philosophers who have touched my life in some way. Tolstoy revealing the workings of history, the need for idealism, the traps (and joys) of sexual passion. Forster bringing home the need for making connections, for keeping proportion, for tolerance ... but only up to a certain point. Sartre stirring up the need for political engagement and de Beauvoir giving me a vocabulary with which to think about my position as a woman. Nabokov encouraging me to frolic in language. Proust wanting me to wallow in *everything*. Woolf sending me inside the minds of others, and American poet e. e. cummings encouraging joy (his world 'mud-luscious' and 'puddle-wonderful'). Calvino changing my vision of what can be done in fiction and the French writer Georges Perec astounding me with the bending of language – a novel without a single 'e', and another with no vowels *but* 'e' (and perhaps the even more prodigious achievement, the translation of those novels by Gilbert Adair). George Eliot making me serious. And Aristophanes ... and Cervantes ... and Gertrude Stein ... and ... All coming to my party – and all obliged to accept the invitation as they could no longer claim pressure of time or work or other commitments: 'time' was something they had plenty of now ... and it was no longer linear, anyway.

The party's in full swing. There's the usual little clusters of those who already know each other and contemporaries talking over their times – Shakespeare casts a cool eye over Christopher Marlowe and is getting on better with Cervantes (the language barrier non-existent thanks to Heaven's own special Esperanto); Proust is still not quite hitting it off with Oscar Wilde, and Gertrude Stein is bristling at another unpleasant remark from Hemingway; George Eliot is being *terribly* earnest with Jane Austen; and Rousseau is still feeling rather sorry for himself (Voltaire and Diderot exchanging winks at his expense …). And so it goes. A positive *mêlée* of beards and baldness, curls and crops, togas, jerkins, cloaks, smocks, frocks, cassocks, cod-pieces, pleats, smoking jackets, cardigans, kilts, crinolines, frock coats, duffle coats, suits, shawls, boas, bonnets, blazers, jeans …

They've arranged a cabaret for me (an idea pinched from my novel, *Zade*): favourite excerpts from books I've loved in life, performed by the writers themselves (except for T. S. Eliot: they seem to know I'd prefer to hear *Four Quartets* read by the voice in my head, not his).

The cabaret is very long – no hurry, here. I have time to look around between 'turns' and take in just how many guests there are. The still-living are absent, of course. (Maybe I'll get myself invited to the welcome parties when *their* times come.) Among the writers I can spot, even at first glance, Æschylus, Alain-Fournier, Anouilh, Aragon, Aristophanes, Auden, Austen, Balzac, Baudelaire, Beckett, Bellow,

Benjamin, Bradbury, Bulgakov, Burgess, Calvino,
Camus, Carter, Cervantes, Chekhov, Cocteau,
Colette, Conrad, e.e.cummings, Dante, Daudet,
de Beauvoir, Dickens, Diderot, Dostoyevsky, Eliot
(George), Eliot (T.S.), Flaubert, Forster, Genet,
Gide, Goethe, Gogol, Goncharov, Gorky, Greene,
Hardy, Hartley, Hemingway, Hugo, Huxley, Isher-
wood, James, Jerome K. Jerome, Johnson (B.S.),
Johnson (Dr.), Joyce, Kafka, La Fontaine, Lawrence,
Lehmann, Levi (Carlo), Levi (Primo), Mann
(Thomas), Mann (Klaus), Mansfield, Marcus Aure-
lius, Maupassant, Melville, Molière, Montaigne,
Moravia, Morris (William), Murdoch, Nabokov,
Orwell, Pagnol, Pasternak, Perec, Powell, Prévert,
Proust, Pym, Queneau, Rabelais, Racine, Rhys,
Robbe-Grillet, Sarraute, Sartre, Sevigné (Madame
de) Shaw, Simon, Smart (Elizabeth), Snow, Spark,
Stein, Stendhal, Stevenson, Strachey, Tolstoy, Twain,
Verlaine, Vian, Voltaire, Vonnegut, Waugh (Evelyn),
Wells, West, White (Antonia), Wilde, Woolf, Zola ...

And now for the last item of the cabaret. It's
performed as a kind of ballet-cum-mime, all wearing
fairy wings (or are they supposed to be angels?), with
a voice-over. It's back to the origins of my love for
books, language, literature, reading, writing ... It's the
voice of my mother casting a protective spell – I'm a
small child again, sitting by her knees as she reads ...

You spotted snakes with double tongue,
Thorny hedgehogs, be not seen.
Newts and blind-worms, do no wrong.
Come not near our Fairy Queen.

   Philomel, with melody
   Sing in our sweet lullaby –
   Lulla, lulla, lullaby; lulla, lulla, lullaby:
   Never harm, nor spell, nor charm
   Come our lovely lady nigh;
   So, good-night, with lullaby.

Weaving spiders, come not here:
Hence, you long-legg'd spinners, hence;
Beetles black, approach not near;
Worm nor snail, do no offence.

   Philomel with melody
   Sing in our sweet lullaby –
   Lulla, lulla, lullaby; lulla, lulla, lullaby:
   Never harm, nor spell, nor charm
   Come our lovely lady nigh;
   So, good-night, with lullaby.

But there's no need to conjure that party in the next world. They're still here, those writers, all of them. I only have to raise my head from my desk and the circus-ring of light from the angle-poise lamp by which I'm writing to see their books on the shelves around me. I can have them all for company and still be with the living as well as the dead.

Malcolm's just called out that he's pouring me a glass of wine.

The party's here. The party's now. And I intend to go on having a great time ...

❧ SELECTED BIBLIOGRAPHY ❧

al-Hamad, Turki *Adama*, Saqi, 2003, translated by Robin Bray; *Shumaisi*, Saqi 2005, translated by Paul Starkey.

Bakewell, Sarah *How to Live: A Life of Montaigne in One Question and Twenty Attempts at an Answer*, Chatto and Windus, 2010.

Barbery, Muriel *L'Élégance du hérisson* Gallimard, 2006. *The Elegance of the Hedgehog*, Gallic Books, 2008; translated by Alison Anderson.

Barnes, Julian *Nothing to be Frightened Of*, Jonathan Cape, 2008.

Benjamin, Walter *The Arcades Project*, The Belknapp Press (Harvard University Press) 1999; Harvard University Press paperback, 2002.

Blom, Philipp *Encyclopédie: The Triumph of Reason in an Unreasonable Age*, Fourth Estate, 2004.

Bloom, Harold *The Western Canon: the Books and School of the Ages,* Harcourt Brace, 1994; Macmillan, 1995.

Bloom, Harold *How to Read and Why,* Fourth Estate, 2000; paperback, 2001.

Bodanis, David *Passionate Minds: The Great Scientific Affair*, Little, Brown, 2006; Abacus, 2007.

Booth, Wayne C. *The Company We Keep: An Ethics of Fiction*, University of California Press, 1988.

Breakwell, Ian and Hammond, Paul *Brought to Book: The Balance of Books and Life*, Penguin, 1995.

Brussig, Thomas *Heroes Like Us* Berlin, 1995; The Harvill Press, 1997; translated by John Brownjohn.

Buzbee, Lewis *The Yellow-Lighted Bookshop*, Graywolf Press, 2006.

Calvino, Italo *Six Memos for the Next Millenium*, Jonathan Cape, 1992; translated by Patrick Creagh.

Calvino, Italo, *Why Read the Classics?*, Italy, 1991; Jonathan Cape, 1999; Vintage edition, 2000; translated by Martin McLaughlin.

Canetti, Elias *Auto da Fé*, Austria, 1935; Jonathan Cape, 1946; translated by C. V. Wedgewood, under the personal supervision of the author.

Cave, Terence *How to Read Montaigne*, Granta Books, 2007.

Cercas, Javier *Soldiers of Salamis*, Spain 2001; Bloomsbury, 2003; translated by Anne McLean (Independent Foreign Fiction Prize).

Coetzee, J. M. *Diary of a Bad Year*, Harvill Secker, 2007.

de Botton, Alain *How Proust Can Change Your Life*, Picador, 1997.

Djemaï, Abdelkader *Gare du Nord*, Seuil, 2003.

Doctorow, E. L. *The March*, Random House, 2005

Eco, Umberto *The Name of the Rose* Italy, 1980; Secker and Warburg, 1983; translated by William Weaver.

Fadiman, Anne *Ex Libris: Confessions of a Common Reader*, Farrar, Straus and Giroux, New York, 1998.

Figes, Eva *Light*, HarperCollins, 1983; Pallas Athene, 2007.

Figes, Eva *Tales of Innocence and Experience*, Bloomsbury, 2003.

Figes, Orlando *Natasha's Dance*, Allen Lane, 2002; Penguin, 2003.

Figes, Orlando *The Whisperers*, Allen Lane, 2007; Penguin, 2008.

Fortey, Richard *LIFE: an unauthorised biography*, Flamingo (HarperCollins), 1998.

French, Marilyn *The Women's Room*, André Deutsch, 1978; Virago, 1997.

Gay, Peter *Modernism: the Lure of Heresy*, W. W. Norton, 2008; Vintage, 2009.

Gessen, Masha *Two Babushkas*, Bloomsbury, 2004.

Gibson, Robert *The End of Youth*, Impress Books, 2005.

Glendinning, Victoria *Leonard Woolf: A Life*, Simon and Schuster, 2006.

Haine, W. Scott *The World of the Paris Café: Sociability among the French Working Class 1789-1914*, John Hopkins University Press, 1996; John Hopkins paperback edition, 1999.

Hamsun, Knut *Hunger*, Denmark, 1890; the best translation (of several) is said to be by Sverre Lyngstad, published by Canongate, 1996.

Kauffman, Jean-Paul *The Dark Room at Longwood: A Voyage to St Helena*, France, 1997; Harvill Press, 1999; translated by Patricia Clancy.

Kemal, Orhan *The Idle Years*, Turkey, 1950; Peter Owen, 2008; translated by Cengiz Lugal.

Kemal, Yashar *The Birds Have Also Gone*, Turkey, 1978; Collins Harvill, 1987; Minerva (Methuen), 1989; translated by Thilda Kemal.

Kincaid, Jamaica *A Small Place*, Putnam, 1989.

Kundera, Milan *The Unbearable Lightness of Being* Czech-oslovakia, 1984; Faber and Faber, 1984: translated from the Czech by Henry Heim.

Le Clézio, J. M. G *Raga: approche du continent invisible,* Seuil, 2006.

Lee, Harper *To Kill a Mockingbird,* William Heinemann, 1960; many subsequent editions.

Lee, Hermione *Edith Wharton,* Chatto and Windus, 2007; Vintage, 2008.

Manguel, Alberto *A Reading Diary,* Knopf, 2004; Canongate, 2005.

Manguel, Alberto *History of Reading,* HarperCollins, 1996; Flamingo, 1997.

Manguel, Alberto *Into the Looking-Glass World,* Bloomsbury, 1999.

Manguel, Alberto, *The City of Words* (CBC Massey Lectures), Anansi, 2007.

Manguel, Alberto *The Library at Night,* Yale University Press, 2006.

Mansel, Philip *Constantinople: City of the World's Desire, 1453-1924,* John Murray, 1995; Penguin, 1997.

Matteson, John *Eden's Outcasts: The Story of Louisa May Alcott and her Father,* W. W. Norton, 2007.

McEwan, Ian *Atonement,* Jonathan Cape, 2001; Vintage, 2002.

McWhorter, John *The Power of Babel,* Arrow Books, 2003.

Mercer, Jeremy *Books, Baguettes and Bedbugs: The Left Bank World of Shakespeare and Co,* Weidenfeld and Nicholson, 2005. Phoenix paperback, 2006.

Midgley, Mary *The Owl of Minerva: A Memoir*, Routledge, 2005.

Morrison, Blake, 'The Reading Cure', *Guardian*, 5/1/2008.

Nabokov, Vladimir *Invitation to a Beheading*, Russia, 1935/6 (serialised); Weidenfeld and Nicolson, 1960; translated by Dmitri Nabokov, under the supervision of the author.

Nabokov, Vladimir *Lolita*, Paris, 1955; New York, 1958; Weidenfeld and Nicolson, 1959; Penguin, 1980 (and many since).

Nabokov, Vladimir *Speak, Memory*, Weidenfeld and Nicolson, 1967; Penguin, 1969.

Nafisi, Azar *Reading Lolita in Tehran: A Memoir in Books*, Random House, 2003.

Nemirovsky, Irène *Suite Française*, France, 2004; Chatto and Windus, 2006; translated by Sandra Smith.

Orsenna, Erik *Le Grammaire est un chanson douce*, Stock, 2001.

Orsenna, Erik *Portrait du Gulf Stream*, Éditions du Seuil, 2005.

Orsenna, Erik *Portrait d'un homme heureux, André Le Nôtre*, Fayard, 2000.

Over, Jeremy see particularly *A Little Bit of Bread and No Cheese* (2001) and *Deceiving Wild Creatures* (2009), both published by Carcanet.

Over, Marita see particularly *Other Lilies* (Frogmore Press, 1997) and *Not Knowing Itself* (Arrowhead Press, 2006).

Pamuk, Orhan *Istanbul: Memories of a City*, Faber and Faber, 2005.

Pamuk, Orhan *Other Colours: Essays and a Story*, Faber and Faber, 2007; translated by Maureen Freely.

Pamuk, Orhan *Snow*, Faber and Faber, 2004; translated by Maureen Freely.

Pasternak, Boris The Childhood of Luvers', translated by Robert Payne, in *Pasternak: Prose and Poems*, Ernest Benn Ltd., London, 1959.

Pennac, Daniel *Chagrin d'école*, Gallimard, 2007.

Pennac, Daniel *Comme un roman,* Gallimard, 1992. Translated by Daniel Gunn as *Reads Like a Novel,* Quartet, London, 1994. Translated by Sarah Adams as *The Rights of the Reader*, Walker Books, 2006.

Pennac, Daniel *The Dictator and the Hammock*, Gallimard, 2003; translated by Patricia Clancy, Harvill Secker, 2006.

Pearson, Roger *Voltaire Almighty: A Life in Pursuit of Freedom*, Bloomsbury, 2005.

Queneau, Raymond *Zazie dans le métro*, Gallimard, 1959; *Zazie in the metro*, Bodleyhead, 1960; John Calder, 1982; Penguin Classics, 2000; translated by Barbara Wright.

Reyes, Heather *Zade*, Saqi Books, 2004.

Robb, Graham *The Discovery of France*, W. W. Norton, 2007; Picador, 2008.

Phyllis Rose *The Year of Reading Proust*, Vintage, 1998.

Sacks, Oliver *Musicophilia* Knopf, 2007; Vintage, 2008.

Sartre, Jean-Paul *Nausea*, Gallimard, 1938; Penguin, 1965, translated by Robert Baldick.

Seirerstad, Åsne *The Bookseller of Kabul*, Norway, 2002; Virago, 2004; translated by Ingrid Christophersen.

Simon, Claude, *Le Jardin des Plantes*, Les Éditions de Minuit, 1997.

Simon, Claude, *La Chevelure de Bérénice*, Éditions de Minuit, 1984.

Spufford, Francis *The Child that Books Built*, Faber and Faber, 2002.

Spurling, Hilary Volume One: *The Unknown Matisse (1869–1908)*, Hamish Hamilton, 1998; Penguin, 2000. Volume Two: *Matisse the Master (1909–1954)*, Hamish Hamilton, 2005; Penguin 2006 (Whitbread Book of the Year 2005).

Troyat, Henri *Aliocha*, Flammarion, 1991.

Troyat, Henri *La Neige en Deuil*, Flammarion, 1952.

Troyat, Henri, *Tolstoy*, Doubleday, 1967; Pelican Books, 1970.

Vian, Boris, *Contes de fées à l'usage des moyennes personnes*, Pauvert, 1996 and 1998.

Vico, Giambattista *Scienza Nuova (The New Science)*, first published, 1725. Available in a translation by Thomas Goddard Bergin and Max Harold Fisch, Cornell University Press, 1968; Cornell Paperback, 1984.

Wall, Geoffrey *Flaubert: A Life*, Faber and Faber, 2001.

Wesker, Arnold, *Roots* 'The Wesker Trilogy', Jonathan Cape, 1960; Penguin Books, 1964 and subsequent editions.

Wolf, Maryanne, *Proust and the Squid: The Story and Science of the Reading Brain*, Icon Books, 2008.

Wood, James *How Fiction Works*, Jonathan Cape, 2008

Woolf, Leonard *The Village in the Jungle* 1913; most recent republishing, Eland, 2010.

Woolf, Virginia *Jacob's Room*, The Hogarth Press, 1922. Many editions since.

∽ INDEX ∾

'Heather Reyes writes with tremendous verve and wit.'
Jill Dawson, Orange Prize shortlisted author
of *Fred & Edie*

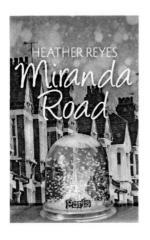

Miranda Road
Heather Reyes

Once she dreamt of literary fame, now Georgina Hardiman just tries to bring up her young daughter Eloisa intelligently – and to stay sane in Thatcher's Britain.

But Eloisa has her own ideas about what she wants from life ... starting with a father.

A visit to Paris brings mother and daughter up against secrets of the past – and starts them both on a journey towards different kinds of happiness.

Miranda Road is a bitter-sweet and wonderfully witty meditation on love, on being a mother and a daughter, and on the difficulties of freeing ourselves from the past.

'Hugely readable and quietly profound, this novel about family in the most modern sense, explores the singular bond between mother and daughter. Set in London and Paris, it explores the aftermath of passion, of political upheaval and of the disintegration of the nuclear family with a sensitivity that is both lyrical and deeply moving.'
Beatrice Colin, Richard and Judy Book Club author of
The Luminous Life of Lily Aphrodite

Available in ebook/print book   £8.99   9780992636418
Oxygen Books